TO' JANGGUT

T0345611

TO' JANGGUT

Legends, Histories, and Perceptions of the 1915 Rebellion in Kelantan

Cheah Boon Kheng

NUS PRESS
SINGAPORE

© Cheah Boon Kheng

Published by:

NUS Press
National University of Singapore
AS3-01-02, 3 Arts Link
Singapore 117569

Fax: (65) 6774-0652
E-mail: nusbooks@nus.edu.sg
Website: http://nuspress.nus.edu.sg

Reprint 2018

ISBN 978-981-32-5000-0 (Paper)

National Library Board, Singapore Cataloguing-in-Publication Data
A catalogue record for the book is available from the National Library, Singapore

The first edition was published by Singapore University Press in 2006.

Typeset by: International Typesetters Pte Ltd
Printed by: Markono Print Media Pte Ltd

Contents

List of Maps

List of Illustrations

Acknowledgements

I am grateful to the staff of several organisations for their assistance during the course of my research, especially those at the Universiti Sains Malaysia Library, the National Archives of Malaysia, the National Archives of Singapore, and the Bodleian and Rhodes House Libraries, in Oxford, England. I would also like to thank two former undergraduate students, Tan Ban Teik and Islas alias Ariffin Ismail, for undertaking To' Janggut's rebellion as coursework assignments for the 1981–2 and 1983–4 history courses I taught at Science University of Malaysia. Tan Ban Teik's essay was later published as part of an occasional paper by the School of Humanities; and Islas' work has been used by history teachers in Kota Bahru. Both students helped me with advice, translations and references. In December 1996 while visiting Kota Bahru to attend a National University of Malaysia seminar on To' Janggut, I was pleased to meet up again with Tan Ban Teik, who assisted me further by accompanying me on a research trip to Pasir Putih.

Thanks also to Nik Haslinda bt. Nik Hussain, a history lecturer at Science University of Malaysia, and to Dr Fatimah Busu, novelist and retired literature Science University of Malaysia lecturer, both Kelantanese, for lending me their personal collections of some rare, old story books (in Jawi script) on To' Janggut. I am also indebted to Dr Tan Liok Ee, my former colleague at the History Department, Science University of Malaysia, in Penang, who while on sabbatical leave at Oxford University in December 1998, acquired on my behalf additional photographic materials on Kelantan at Rhodes House Library. She warmheartedly e-mailed me her impressions of the photographic materials, a number of her comments have been included in this book. The Bodleian Library assisted in the reproduction of several photographs for publication. Drafts of this book were presented at a seminar at the Australian National University in Canberra in 1998. Many of those present at the seminar gave me useful advice and comments, especially Anthony Diller and Virginia Matheson Hooker, for which I thank them. I would like to thank the Malaysian Branch of the Royal Asiatic Society for permission to reproduce two articles of mine on To' Janggut which were published in the society's journal in 1995 and 1999 and appear in this book in a revised form.

In addition, I would like to thank two anonymous reviewers whose comments and suggestions about my original manuscript helped shape my thinking about this book in its final form. Dr Paul H. Kratoska, Director of NUS Publishing, deserves special mention and my gratitude for the attention and care he devoted to my manuscript. Owing to his own interest in To' Janggut's history, he took on the additional duty of copy-editor and offered useful advice and comments about revisions that helped to sharpen my focus. Our friendship dates back to 1978–88 when Paul taught at Science University of Malaysia, and we share many common interests, including food, popular culture and peasant rebellions. My sincere thanks also to editor Danielle McClellan (formerly of the Monthly Review) who refined and improved the final draft. Finally, I would like to thank Science University of Malaysia for offering me a visiting professorship in 2004–5 at its School of Humanities and for providing me with office space, library privileges and a stimulating environment in which to complete this book. While there I presented a seminar on To' Janggut and am grateful for the comments, support and encouragement that I received from colleagues, including members of the History Department and the School of Social Sciences.

Introduction

This book is about a charismatic local Malay leader known as "To'*Janggut" (Old Long Beard), who staged a rebellion against British rule in the Malayan state of Kelantan in the early twentieth century, and about various accounts of his uprising. In the pages that follow, the "Romance of To' Janggut" appears in several versions, each drawn from a different source — including scholarly interpretations, literary and folk accounts, newspaper reports, photographs, and "hidden" secret and confidential official papers. An examination of this palimpsest reveals ever deepening layers of To' Janggut's rebellion, much as the Japanese film director Akira Kurosawa's film *Rashomon* shows a murder through the eyes of seven individuals, each of whom saw the event differently.

Another model for this book is the French historian Emmanuel Le Roy Ladurie's *Love, Money and Death in the Pays D'oc* (New York: Penguin Books, 1980), a fascinating, bold and imaginative account that bridges the gap between folk literature and history, between fiction and fact. Ladurie's book examines a popular love story set in rural France that is known to many French-speaking peoples throughout the world. In writing it, he tracked down some 320 different versions of the tale, and through a penetrating analysis of 50 "key" stories along with their variations, and other Occitan oral literature, illuminated not only the content and structures of oral fiction, but also the society and customs of the peasant populations of the Pays d'Oc in the eighteenth century.

I have also drawn on the work of a variety of scholars doing work in textual analysis and alternative historical genres, especially Timothy Lindsey [*The Romance of K'tut Tantri and Indonesia* (Kuala Lumpur: Oxford University Press, 1997)], and Lorraine M. Gesick, whose study

---

* "To'" is pronounced to rhyme with "broke".

of a southern Thai folk legend and its several versions is presented in her book *In the Land of Lady White Blood: Southern Thailand and the Meaning of History* (Ithaca, NY: Southeast Asia Programme, Cornell University, 1995).

I begin by presenting the outlines of the story of To' Janggut's rebellion, limiting my account to a bare statement of the facts that are corroborated by all versions of the event. This is followed by an indigenous oral folk account of the Kelantan rising, *Peperangan To' Janggut atau Balasan Derhaka* in translation, with a brief commentary that explains how this version of the 1915 rising differs from the official Malay and British accounts of the rising.

In the second part of the book, I contrast elements within this folk account with later versions of the event found in newspaper reports, photographs, and a collection of official documents classified "confidential" and "secret", and only recently made available to the public. In these versions, incidents and images associated with the folk account are variously revised, contradicted, and denied. Many of the materials — memoirs, correspondence and reports written by To' Janggut's contemporaries — are stored in government archives. The stories they contain are unknown to the general reading public, and their presentation in this book along with my own interpretations of events constitutes yet another version of the rising, a new and composite one that differs in many particulars from previous accounts.

In the end the mystery of To' Janggut remains unresolved. The deconstruction or reconstruction of each incident constitutes an act of interpretation and is a form of argumentation. Although we cannot know the "truth" of what actually happened, by comparing and through the interaction of different versions and texts, we can ascertain the goals, beliefs and perspectives embodied in the sources. The "truth" of these new versions is no less problematic than the truth of those that preceded them, and readers are left to form their own speculative histories of the events of 1915 in Kelantan.

Cheah Boon Kheng
Penang, 6 September 2005

Part I

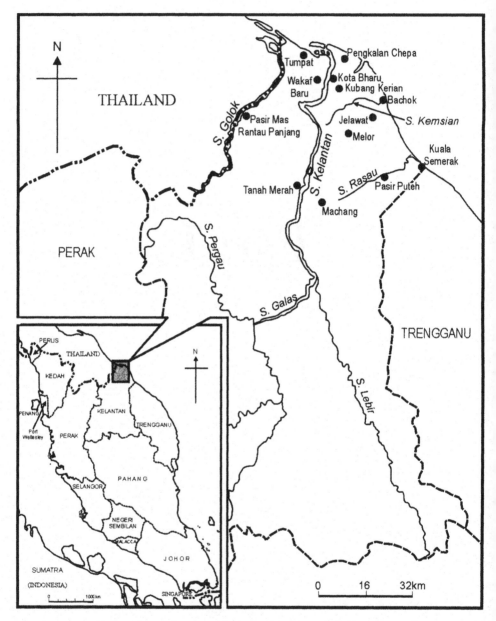

Map of Kelantan

Chapter 1

History, Politics and Society, and To' Janggut's Rebellion in Kelantan

I found, as did also Mr Pepys, [the District Officer responsible for Pasir Putih] an extraordinary difficulty in getting any cause alleged for the rising.

> — W. Langham-Carter,
> British Adviser to the Sultan of Kelantan,
> in a memorandum to the
> Governor in Singapore, 12 July 1915

What we must normally do is to put together a wide variety of often fragmentary information; and to do that we must, if you'll excuse the phrase, construct the jigsaw puzzle ourselves, that is work out how such information *ought* to fit together.

> — British historian Eric Hobsbawm
> on historical methodology in his book
> *On History*[1] [emphasis added]

Introduction

The 1915 rising at Pasir Putih in Kelantan has attracted substantial scholarly attention, but there is little agreement among researchers about the basic facts of the rising, or its causes. The puzzle has not been assembled, and it is possible that the pieces cannot be fit together. Each assessment of the rebellion depends very much on the kind of questions asked, and on the sources available to the researcher. Some scholars have used identical evidence to arrive at differing interpretations, while others have presented new evidence that challenges and contradicts existing interpretations.

Scholarly writings portray the rising in a number of ways: It has been seen as (a) a direct protest against British administration after the state had come under British protection in 1909; (b) an indirect protest against the Sultan for accepting British protection and as an attempt to oust him; (c) a product of strong provincial sentiment in favour of a local feudal lord, Ungku Besar, and against non-Kelantanese, in particular the District Officer (D.O.) of Pasir Putih, a Singapore Malay named Abdul Latif who was seen as having usurped Ungku Besar's powers; (d) a peasant rebellion against new land taxes and the allegedly harsh methods used by the D.O. to collect taxes; and (e) a *jihad* (holy war) against Britain following the outbreak of the First World War, in which the United Kingdom was part of an alliance of European powers fighting against Germany, Austria and Turkey — the latter an Islamic nation whose religious leader had called on Muslims all over the world to support Turkey's side in the war. These assessments have found their way into school and university history textbooks used in Malaysia, and have helped to create a romantic legend around To' Janggut and his struggle.

Another account of To' Janggut's story has flourished outside the classroom, a folk version of his struggle that survives in the region of Kelantan where he lived. This account, which provides a very different interpretation of To' Janggut's story and of Malay resistance in Kelantan, contains elements that were suppressed from public official accounts, but are confirmed by information in formerly closed archival records.

The varying reports of the rebellion and the numerous interpretations of the underlying meaning and motivation of its participants highlight different aspects of the event and different motives for the actors involved. However, certain basic information about To' Janggut's rebellion is uncontested, and appears in all iterations of the story.

Before turning to the various versions of events and the motives that underlie these different accounts, it will be useful to look briefly at the history of the region to understand the landscape where the events occurred.

THE REBELLION AT PASIR PUTIH, 1915
A Time Line of Events

29 April 1915. At a public meeting to discuss the new land tax in Jeram a police sergeant attempts to arrest To' Janggut, but is stabbed to death. This marks the start of the rebellion. On learning that a band of rebels is moving towards Pasir Putih town, the District Officer (D.O.) of Pasir Putih, Abdul Latif, flees with his family, taking with him all the money in the Treasury. Before departing he sends a message overland to the British Adviser in Kota Bahru. The rebels occupy Pasir Putih town, ransack government buildings and burn down several shophouses. The British Adviser receives the D.O.'s letter at 8 p.m. A few hours later a party of Sikh and Malay police leaves for Juaran, 18 miles away, a place situated half-way between Kota Bahru and Pasir Putih.

30 April. News is received that some 5,000 rebels are advancing towards the capital. The Sultan of Kelantan sends two Malay ministers to arrest To' Janggut and restore order, and meanwhile doubles the guard at the palace in Kota Bahru. The British Adviser sends a telegram informing the Governor in Singapore of the outbreak, and orders the evacuation of European women and children to safety at a European estate in southern Thailand. European estate managers in Pasir Putih abandon their bungalows and make their way to Kota Bahru. After their departure, the bungalows are looted.

1 May. The Governor in Singapore receives the British Adviser's telegram asking for immediate military assistance. In Kelantan a group of Malay ministers hold talks with the rebels near Pasir Putih.

3 May. British troops leave Singapore by ship for Kota Bahru. In Kelantan the Sultan of the neighbouring state of Trengganu begins an official visit, and the Malay ministers bring back a demand from the rebels for a full pardon as a condition of halting the rebellion. The Sultan rejects this demand.

5 May. British troops disembark at Tumpat.

6 May. British troops arrive at Gunong. Some troops are said to have been fired on in Pasir Mas.

7 May. A British man-of-war anchored at the mouth of the Semerak River fires shells in the direction of Pasir Putih, but they do not hit the town. The Sultan of Trengganu departs for home.

9 May. British troops enter Pasir Putih town, but rebels have dispersed.

12 May. A military force, the Malay States Guides (Sikh Regiment), arrives from Singapore to relieve the British troops.

15 May. British troops return to Singapore.

24 May. To' Janggut's forces attack the Malay States Guides in Pasir Putih. In the exchange of fire, To' Janggut is killed along with two other rebels. His body is brought back to Kota Bahru, where it is placed on a bullock cart and carried around the town for the public to see. The body is then suspended from a wooden gibbet for an hour at a public field before being taken across the river for burial in Pasir Pekan. Meanwhile, the hunt for any remaining rebels continues.

The State of Kelantan and Its Administration
Kelantan's Transitional Phase, 1902–9

In the Kelantan rising of 1915, although resistance was localised, the traditional leaders — chiefs, aristocrats and the ruler — were all engaged in making a last-ditch stand against the loss of their privileges. The peasant "masses" joined the resistance, largely as a result of customary obedience to these leaders. To understand their role in the Kelantan uprising, we will look at why and how the leaders' traditional privileges had been gradually eroded even before Kelantan came formally under British protection in 1909, and the bitterness and hostility that this aroused.

In 1902, the state's transition from tradition to modernity was already under way. The state had come under the administration of two British officers, W.A. Graham and H.W. Thomson, appointed by Siam as its Adviser and Assistant Adviser respectively to the Raja (later retitled Sultan) of Kelantan. This had been done under an agreement signed that year between Siam and Britain that allowed Britain some degree of control over Kelantan, while the state remained nominally under Siam. Before this, in 1900, the Raja of Kelantan had leased to a British entrepreneur, R.W. Duff, 1,904 square miles of land — practically one-third of the state — and had granted Duff a monopoly over all mineral, trading and other rights within the concession. This agreement was motivated by the ruler's eagerness for quick financial returns and marked the beginning of European exploitation of Kelantan's rich mineral resources. The 1902 treaty initiated a series of reforms in financial and administrative matters, and Graham's administration recovered the leased territory from the Duff syndicate.

Territory, Feudalism and the Border with Trengganu

Since the middle of the eighteenth century, Kelantan's political situation had been unstable. The state had been broken up into several feudatory chiefdoms under the sway of Patani or Trengganu, two states treated by Siam as being on an equal footing.[2] While relations with Siam were uneasy, several feudal chiefs had carved out small "states", such as Limbat, Jeram and Kubang Labu where they ruled like petty monarchs. Even on the Patani side, Graham noted, there were seven tiny "states". In 1776 Long Yunus, with the assistance of Trengganu forces, captured Kota Kubang Labu from the ruler of Legih, inaugurating a ruling dynasty that remains on the throne to this day. Under Long Yunus, who died in 1794, local chiefs were more or less subdued. Limbat later ceased to exist as a feudatory state, and was incorporated into Kelantan proper. To maintain friendly relations with Siam, Kelantan began sending the *bunga mas* — a miniature golden tree — triennially to Bangkok.

In the midst of a short civil war during the nineteenth century,[3] an authoritarian ruler emerged in the person of Sultan Senik (1838–77), who was universally known as *Sultan Mulut Merah* or the "Sultan with the red mouth". During his reign Kelantan grew in strength and prosperity, but in his old age he became short-tempered and ruled his people with harshness, inflicting capital punishment frequently and practising mutilation as a penalty for theft.[4] Sultan Senik introduced a system of registration of all changes of land tenure, by which means land purchased or inherited was recognised as the property of the registering party. His son, who succeeded him, ruled with wisdom and moderation, but his death triggered a succession dispute among his sons. The son chosen by Siam as his successor, Sultan Ahmad, died mysteriously after a short reign. The next ruler, Sultan Mansur, created a land office to maintain land registers and issue title deeds. When Graham arrived to take over the administration in 1903, he found an "advanced system of land registration, which, indeed, requires little alteration to render it thoroughly satisfactory".[5]

Political Intrigues

When Sultan Mansur died in February 1900, his nephew, Tuan Long Senik, succeeded him, with Siamese backing. Tuan Long Senik was not well received by his uncles and members of the Kelantan royal family. "Seven of the most powerful of his uncles and other relatives formed a league by the strength of which combination they extracted from him privileges to which, without such cohesion, they could never have aspired," said Graham.[6] Sultan Senik became practically powerless in the hands of his relatives. They insisted that he consult them on all matters of state, and be allowed to veto his orders if they thought fit. They also accumulated large estates in land, the taxes for which they systematically failed to pay, and protected large numbers of noted evil-doers from whose unconcealed crimes they derived pecuniary and other benefits. One of these uncles, Tuan Long Jaafar, or Tungku Petra, had claimed the throne but had been passed over, and bore a grudge against the ruler. Other notables were also dissatisfied, including Tungku Chik Penambang, a descendant of an earlier Sultan who had not been selected for the post of second-ranking ruler, or Raja Muda.

Graham's Reforms

Upon becoming Siamese Adviser in 1903, Graham had to contend with the state's political and economic problems. The reforms he introduced reaffirmed the status of the Sultan and created an organised administration. He reorganised and restructured the government services, and created a number of new departments, including a State Treasury, where proper registers of receipts and payments were kept. State revenues, which were practically non-existent in 1902, amounted to $320,000 by 1907. To preserve law and order he transformed the existing police force into a well-organised, responsible and efficient service. A new Central Police Station was built in Kota Bahru in 1904. Finally, penal, civil and revenue enactments were passed, and by 1905 a High Court of the Raja along with central and small Courts in Kota Bahru were hearing cases, operating alongside the *syariah* court.

Graham established formal boundaries in rural areas, replacing existing districts. The state was initially divided into five new districts, namely Kota Bharu, Batu Mengkebang (later known as Ulu Kelantan), Pasir Putih, Kuala Kelantan, and Kuala Lebir, but only the first three of these came into existence. Each district was placed under a district officer who also acted as magistrate, land officer and revenue collector.

Before these reforms, the Sultan, nobles and their relatives had exclusive rights over state revenue, but under the new system, the Sultan agreed to content himself with what was apportioned to him by the state and leave the remaining revenue to the management of the state treasurer. Following these reforms, the relatives of the Raja who had earlier conspired against him began to accept the new situation.[7] In order to make them a peaceful, contented and useful element in the development of the state, Graham appointed many of the relatives to positions as heads of the newly established or reorganised government departments. For their part, they cooperated and worked the system. They were assisted in the management of affairs either by British or Siamese officers who had been recruited to the state services from 1903. Of the seven "uncles", Tungku Petra Didalam Kebun (Phra Pitak) was regarded by Graham as "most trustworthy", and his work while in temporary charge of the Police was regarded as "most satisfactory".

Graham next focused his attention on curtailing the powers of the Duff Development Company, which he considered excessive. Following negotiations in Bangkok, the company signed a new agreement in 1905 that abrogated practically all the administrative rights that it held, thereby reducing it to a purely commercial concern. The company began litigation against the governments of Kelantan and Siam at the end of 1907 for the recovery of losses incurred, and was informed that negotiations were underway to bring Kelantan under British protection. This was done in 1909, and in 1912 the Kelantan government purchased the concession for 300,000 pounds sterling, a sum advanced by the Federated Malay States.[8]

The transfer of Kelantan from Thai to British jurisdiction took place under the Anglo-Siamese Treaty of 1909. The Raja of Kelantan was not consulted during the negotiations, and was informed of the change in a letter by the King of Siam. The first Adviser to the Raja of Kelantan under the new regime, J.S. Mason, took over the administration of the state from Graham on 15 July. On 26 October 1910 the Raja of Kelantan signed a treaty giving Britain formal control of Kelantan's foreign relations. The ruler also agreed to appoint a British Adviser and "to follow and give effect to the advice of the Adviser ... in all matters of administration other than those touching the Mohammedan religion and Malay custom". In the following year, 1911, the British formally recognised Tuan Long Senik as ruler with the title of Sultan, and he reigned thenceforth as Sultan Muhammad IV.

District Administration, 1903–15

Graham had appointed officers in different parts of the state to supervise the district and village chiefs, known as *Tok Kweng* and *Tok Nebeng*, respectively. These Siamese titles remained in use until 1917 when they were replaced by the Malay titles of *penggawa* and *penghulu kampung*. Their duties included drawing up lists for the collection of various taxes and determining what each plot of padi should pay, and also the number of coconut trees or durian trees to be taxed, with the money collected channeled through the district office into the State Treasury. They were also given powers and duties to curb crimes. Thus, power in the districts now shifted from the traditional chiefs to the district officer.

With regard to land administration, Graham in 1908 had introduced a system of "grant" and "sale" to differentiate lands that were gifts of the Sultan from those which changed ownership by mutual consent. After the British assumed control of the state, Mason adopted Graham's scheme, improving the procedure for registering transfers of land ownership and issuing certificates of ownership. He also introduced regulations declaring that land left uncultivated for three years would revert to the state, and prohibiting the sale of land to foreigners except with the approval of the State Executive Council.

Mason's successor as British Adviser, J.E. Bishop, transferred hearings of complaints on land matters from the civil courts to the Land Office. When W. Langham-Carter became British Adviser, a comprehensive land register was compiled for the first time to enable the government to have all the names of land-owners in the state, to collect land revenues in a systematic way and to encourage rice cultivation by the peasants. He followed up with the introduction of a new system under which land taxes were based on four classes of land. All land-owners had to pay land-rent, whether they worked their land or not. The new procedures came into effect on 1 January 1915.

These reforms[9] were not well received by the large landowners, who were mostly the aristocrats and members of the royal family, including the Sultan himself, his "seven uncles" and other relatives. The new law was an impediment to land ownership for members of the upper classes, as the Sultan himself found out when he asked that 3,000 acres of land to be exempted from payment of land-rent, and was told that the request could not be granted. Langham-Carter insisted that he had to pay at least $1,800 land-rent a year on this parcel. The Sultan protested, arguing that this particular piece of land was owned by his family and was his rightful inheritance, but he eventually capitulated and agreed to pay. Similarly, the second-ranking ruler, the Raja Kelantan, and the third-ranking ruler, the Raja Muda, had to pay land-rent on the lands they owned.

A meeting held in April 1915 at the Land Office shortly before the outbreak of the rising, which was convened by Langham-Carter at the request of these aristocrats, showed the extent of their concern. Chaired by the Sultan, the meeting asked Langham-Carter to provide further explanation of the implications of the new Land Law. He told the meeting that the administration would not stop the implementation of the law. At the suggestion of the aristocrats he agreed to make slight amendments on the tax rates, but these did not in any way alter the broad outline of the legislation.

The land tax was intended to replace the produce tax paid by *ra'ayat*, the ordinary people in Kelantan, but this was not properly explained. People viewed the land rents as an extra burden imposed by the British administration, and joined the upper classes in opposing the new system. It is significant that in the attack on Pasir Putih town, one of their first actions was to throw out all the land files and burn them.

W.G. Maxwell, who investigated the causes of the rebellion, compared the new land rates with the old produce taxes, and concluded that the new taxes were "decidedly heavier".[10] The produce taxes were paid as follows: padi-tax (A) was assessed upon padi-fields planted from nurseries; it was calculated upon the basis of local systems of measurement but corresponded to a rate of 93¾ cents per cultivated acre; padi tax (B) was assessed upon padi-fields sown directly with seed, and corresponded to 46¾ cents per cultivated acre. Under this system there was no tax on uncultivated land, on land where the crop failed, or on land used for nurseries. Produce taxes also included a levy of 3 cents per annum on every coconut tree in bearing, a levy of 12½ cents per annum on every durian tree in bearing; and a levy of one cent per annum upon every betel vine in bearing.

The new land-tax was collected at the following annual rates: $1 to $1.20 per acre for 1st class land; 80 cents per acre for 2nd class land; 60 cents per acre for 3rd class land; and 40 cents per acre for 4th class land. The new rules provided that when new land was taken up, remission of rent (that is, of the land tax) might be granted for a period not exceeding five years.

Class A rice fields under the old system became either 1st class or 2nd class land under the new system, and Class "B" fields became either 3rd or 4th class land. Maxwell commented:

> It will be seen therefore that the tax per acre upon 2nd or 4th class padi-land is less under the new system than it was under the old system, whilst the tax upon 1st class and 3rd class land is higher. The crux, however, is that under the new system, the land proprietor has to pay in respect of his padi land whether he cultivates it or not, whereas under the old system this was not so. He has also to pay upon land used for nurseries, and to pay whether his crop has been a failure or not. Similarly, in respect of the land covered by his coconut, durian and betel-leaf trees, he has to pay whether the trees are in bearing or not. Again under the old system, land given up to the cultivation of any trees, other than those specified above, was exempt from taxation. This is not so now. In addition to the land-tax, there is a scale of fees for the preparation of land-titles (which are at present practically non-existent) and another scale for survey-fees.[11]

Maxwell added that from the Government point of view, the land-tax was undoubtedly preferable to the produce-tax, and there was no intention of abandoning it.

Why Was the Rising Confined to Pasir Putih?

While Ulu Kelantan had a European District Officer, T.S. Adams, Pasir Putih had a Kelantanese District Officer, Encik Ibrahim. The Kota Bahru district office came under the jurisdiction of the British Adviser. In 1910, Encik Ibrahim resigned. His post was temporarily filled by Encik Leh, head clerk of the High Court. After a year, Encik Latif, a Singaporean, replaced him. Under Encik Latif's predecessors, especially the last one, Pasir Putih's administration and tax collection had been lax. Encik Latif was, however, a strict administrator, and enforced taxation without any exemption. According to one source,

> From about 1913 he had exploited possibilities for revenue collection to the full, going so far as to auction contracts to collect turtle eggs, and even a type of grass called *kerchut*, in several places in the district, simply to increase revenue, for which permission was granted by the British Adviser. These measures enraged those who had hitherto been collecting these products free.[12]

Why did the rising occur mainly in one district, Pasir Putih, and not in the other two districts? The proximity of Pasir Putih to the frontier with the neighbouring state of Trengganu might have been an important factor. It was not an ethnographic frontier nor one based on geography, such as mountains or rivers. It was simply an "artificial" frontier that separated two sovereign states that demanded separate political loyalties. The subjects of these sovereign states knew where the political authority of one began and the other ended. In the eighteenth century Long Yunus established a dynasty in Kelantan with the assistance of Trengganu royalty, but thereafter he distanced himself from his former patrons. He had planted a walking stick into the ground to indicate where his area of sovereignty began in Kota Bharu, but no real attempt was made to demarcate the Kelantan-Trengganu boundary until the advent of British rule.[13]

Located 30 miles from the capital, Kota Bahru, Pasir Putih town is situated a few miles up the Semerak River in south-eastern Kelantan. In 1915 a packed-earth road fit for light motor traffic in dry weather had been established between Kota Bharu and Gunong, about half the distance to Pasir Putih. The remainder of the journey had to be made across the padi fields, which were a sheet of water in the wet season. The usual means of transportation to the state capital was by water, traveling downriver and then along the coast. There was no telegraph link with the district. In 1915 Pasir Putih district had three police stations: Pasir Putih with sixteen men, Kuala Semerak with eight, and Bachok eight. The number of registered fire-arms in the district was 216.[14] Graham reported in 1908 that the population of Pasir Putih town was about 1,000. In the 1911 census the entire Pasir Putih district had a population of 25,525, less than 10 per cent of the total of 286,751 for the entire state. Its revenue for 1914 was only about $24,000 compared with a total state revenue of $726,772. While most of the local Malays were private padi and coconut cultivators and cattle-rearers, some worked as labourers on the few European-owned coconut estates in the district.

The long border with Trengganu provided easy access to refuge in another state for anyone running foul of the law. During the rising, droves of fugitives fled to Besut, the nearest border town on the

Trengganu side, many taking their cattle with them. The authorities in Kelantan had to order them to return out of fear that the district would run short of padi-cultivators and tax-payers. It was initially rumoured, but later found to be untrue, that two elephant loads of ammunition had been sent to the rebels in Pasir Putih from Trengganu.[15] The source of the rumour was unknown, but it is indicative of the close rapport among people on both sides of the border.

Pasir Putih, which had a greater population of padi cultivators than other parts of the state, was also a notorious haven for cattle thieves and gamblers. Between 1800 and 1900 Pasir Putih was known as Pengkalan Limbungan (a harbour with a dry dock) because it was a place for making large boats and sailing prahus. Gradually it acquired a reputation as a gambling town, and there were regular bull- and cock-fights until 1909, when the state opened a district office and a police station to curb these activities and establish law and order.[16]

At the time of the British takeover in 1909, the feudatory chiefdom of Jeram, a rival of Pasir Putih, had barely survived under a petty ruler, Ungku Besar. He was a large landowner, and said to be the grandson of the previous ruler of the district, Tungku Seri Maharaja (Engku Demong bin Engku Seri).[17] Under the new tax regime introduced by the British administration in 1915, he was required to pay land-taxes, from which he had been previously exempted. Ungku Besar resented this change and began to instigate the padi cultivators to resist, plotting with them against the district authority and especially the new land tax system. Either he was unaware of the real intentions behind the reform, or he deliberately suggested that the produce taxes imposed previously were being increased by a fixed land rent. Apparently Encik Latif himself failed to inform the population of the true nature of the change, and for this oversight the British Adviser, W. Langham-Carter, was later held responsible.[18] In the absence of a clear explanation to the contrary, the new system was seen as an added burden on the people, and a new one on members of the aristocracy, who had been exempt from land rent in the past because they did not cultivate their land. "The sudden implementation of the new system in Pasir Puteh by Encik Latif obviously amounted to rubbing salt in the wound he had already inflicted on the people by his alleged harshness," said one source.[19]

R.J. Farrer, who later took over from Langham-Carter as Acting British Adviser, said he thought there was a "general feeling of mild discontent prevalent throughout Kelantan".

> The fact that this discontent has broken out into action at Pasir Putih may be put down to Ungku Besar, To' Janggut, and their followers. The first named is the grandson of Ungku Seliah. To' Janggut was one of the grandfather's right hand men, and has for years been acquiring a reputation as a desperado, and leader of thieves. These men have for some months been sounding people, and holding meetings in the up-country with a view to the establishment of Ungku Besar in his grandfather's position, holding forth as an inducement to *raiats* [the people] the promise of the expulsion of all foreigners (the term includes all non-Kelantanese), and reversion to the old order of things. The murder of the sergeant by To' Janggut merely precipitated matters by a few days.[20]

The Killing of To' Janggut, and Public Display of His Corpse

Before presenting the alternate versions of the 1915 rebellion, let me conclude this chapter with a brief episode of how To' Janggut was killed and what the authorities did to his corpse, which has been revealed in three British private accounts, of which two were by eye-witnesses to the incident. This episode of who among the British officials were involved in the killing and what was done to his corpse is not narrated in any British government report, as apparently attempts were made by the authorities to suppress the news, for the reasons that are made clear more fully in Chapter 7. The British private accounts have been written up only after 12, 40 and 50 years, respectively, after the rebellion. Besides these accounts, the only other source to reveal information about the public display of the corpse in greater detail is the local folk legend.

I wish to stress that the British private accounts confirm and highlight an important episode, which has been completely omitted from the government records and which has consequently been given little attention in the academic studies of the rebellion. As to the events they narrate, these accounts will serve as inter-texts to the version in the local legend, which will be presented in the next chapter. They will be seen to verify, revise, or contradict one another. For instance, while the British private accounts present a rather unflattering picture of To' Janggut as a murderer or fugitive who was hunted down and shot dead, the folk legend romanticises him as a freedom fighter with heroic qualities. The British administration's public display of the corpse, which was endorsed by the Sultan, may have given rise to a free play of the Kelantanese people's imagination on what they thought was the true nature of the rebellion and led them to invent the image of To' Janggut as a folk hero. In fact, the lack of transparency on the part of the British administration on much of the incidents surrounding To' Janggut may be said to have led to some of the ambiguities and doubts in people's minds about the true nature of the rebellion.

The rebellion began when To' Janggut killed a police sergeant on 29 April and almost a month later, on 24 May, To' Janggut himself was killed. His death brought the rebellion to a close, as the remaining rebels fled into hiding. Senior British officials such as Langham-Carter and W.G. Maxwell took part in the final skirmish and exchange of fire between the rebel and government forces. The first private account to describe the episode was published in 1927 in a book by Carveth Wells, who served as a railroad engineer in Pasir Mas district, Kelantan during the rising.

Wells wrote: "When news of these disturbances reached the ears of the Singapore Government, the Hon. George Maxwell was sent to investigate. After visiting me at Pasir Mas, he decided to pay a visit to Pasir Puteh and find out personally whether Tok Janggut was really invulnerable or whether his survival for so long was merely due to rotten shooting.... Shortly afterward I was told that he was walking across a ricefield on his way to Pasir Puteh when the Malays led by Tok Janggut opened fire, and that Maxwell himself shot Tok Janggut successfully which, if correct, is not surprising, as Maxwell is one of the finest big-game shots in the world."[21] Wells then reported that one morning, a car pulled outside the rest-house in Kota Bharu where he was, and the driver urged those inside to come out to take a look at what was at the back of the car: "...tied on the trunk carrier, was the ghastly body of Tok Janggut! As soon as the Sultan heard that the rebel was really dead, he ordered him to be exhibited on a gibbet, suspended by his feet, as an object lesson to others."[22]

Another account published only in 1950 by W.E. Pepys,[23] who had arrived in Kelantan with the Malay States Guides as their political officer and who later took over the job of District Officer from the discredited Abdul Latif, narrates how on the night of 23 May, he, Maxwell, Langham-Carter and a police inspector named Jackson had joined the Malay States Guides (comprising Sikhs under Indian Army British officers) in Pasir Putih. By about 3 a.m. they had been awakened by shots fired into the former district officer's quarters, where the Guides were staying. To' Janggut and his followers, presumably spurred by the Sultan's proclamation calling on the ringleaders to surrender and by the destruction of their houses, had decided to carry the conflict into the enemy's camp. The officers and men of the Guides advanced towards Kampong Jeram, and both sides began firing at each other. The engagement lasted about ten minutes, at the end of which two Sikh soldiers were injured, and the firing from Kampong Jeram ceased. As the British party charged in, they found seven corpses behind a hedge. Among them was To' Janggut, "a venerable-looking bearded gentleman" close to an elephant gun. When they lifted the sarong from his body, they found it had unmistakable evidence of elephantiasis. As To' Janggut had the reputation of being invulnerable, it was decided to send his body to the capital, and this was done the same night. "On its arrival, the Sultan ordered it to be carried across to the old execution ground on the far bank of the Kelantan River, and there to be crucified upside down," wrote Pepys.[24]

The third account, written down in 1966 among his unpublished papers by A.G. Morkill, a police officer and magistrate who also took part during the rising, gave the following details:

> A man fired at Langham-Carter from 30 yards and missed him. L.C. was in great form and killed his man. He behaved as if he was out snipe-shooting. To' Janggut's body was sent to Kota Bahru in a car and exposed for all to see. Since he had made people believe he had a stomach upon which bullets had no effect, H.H. [His Highness the Sultan] as a proof of his "loyalty" requested that the corpse should be hung up by the feet for four hours, which was done, much to the scandalisation of the Secretariat.[25]

The "secretariat" apparently refers Malay members of the government's administrative staff, who were scandalised. The length of time the corpse was left hanging has been a matter of dispute, with some observers saying one hour, others three days. In my opinion, it was probably an hour at the most, because Muslim burials must take place within a day after death, and Muslim Malay opinion would have been outraged at a prolonged desecration of a corpse. This episode generated much sympathy for To' Janggut, and helped create the popular legend surrounding his life and death.

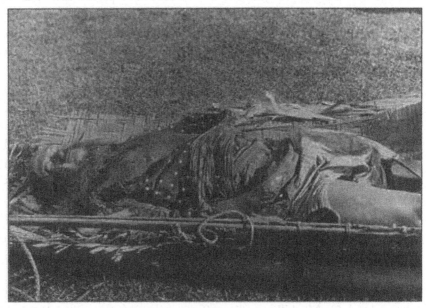

The Corpse of To' Janggut at Padang Bank in Kota Bharu, 1915 [?]

This photograph labelled MS.IND.OCN.S.67 in the A.G. Morkill Collection at the Rhodes House Library, Oxford, United Kingdom is believed to be that of the corpse of To' Janggut after it had been brought to Kota Bharu for public display from Pasir Putih by Indian troops, who had carried it in a bamboo and matted stretcher. The display, made on the Sultan of Kelantan's orders, is believed to have been done at the behest of the British Police Officer G. Jackson and was intended to demolish the myth of To' Janggut's alleged invulnerability. He was believed to have been *kebal* (invulnerable). Note the wound marks on the right hand and on the chest. I acknowledge with thanks the permission of the Bodleian Library, Oxford to reproduce this photograph. Morkill performed several duties in Kelantan in 1915 such as land officer, magistrate and police officer. His private papers, which are deposited at the Rhodes House Library, unfortunately do not provide any caption to the above photograph, so a definitive identification is not possible. (Copyright Bodleian Library, Oxford, U.K.)

Chapter 2

Sources and Interpretations of To' Janggut's History: A Bibliographic Essay

Introduction

To write another history of To' Janggut involves consideration of how other, earlier and conflicting histories were written, and the way in which his legend had been constructed by those histories. This section surveys the principal sources which have been used to evaluate the story of To' Janggut. The literature on To' Janggut is quite extensive, but here I shall identify the main publications and in some cases the principal sources their authors have used, and how they have interpreted his story and legend.

The Works of Kelantanese and Other Malay Writers

The following books by Kelantanese and other Malay writers (presented chronologically) are the major local sources of To' Janggut's legend and the 1915 rebellion: Yahya Abdullah, *Peperangan To' Janggut, atau Balasan Derhaka* (To' Janggut's War, or the Retribution for Rebellion) (Kota Bharu: Muslim Printing Press, 1955); Abdullah b. Amirah Seling Kelantan, *Riwayat Hidup To' Janggut dan Peperangannya di Kelantan* (The Life of To' Janggut and His War) (Penang: Sinaran Brothers, 1957); Arifin bin Abdul Rashid, *Peristiwa-peristiwa di Kelantan* (Events in Kelantan) (Kota Bharu: Muslim Printing Press, 1960); Saad Shukri Haji Muda, *Sejarah Kelantan* (A History of Kelantan) (Kota Bharu: Penerbit Kelantan, 1962); Arifin bin Abdul Rashid, *Ringkasan Sejarah Kelantan* (An Abbreviated History of Kelantan) (Kota Bharu: Al-Ahliah Press, 1962); A. Jalil Haji Noor, *Tok Janggot Pahlawan Kelantan* (Tok Janggut, A Warrior of Kelantan) (Singapore: Pustaka Nasional, 1966);

Mohd. Hashim Khalin Haji Awang, *Kelantan dari zaman ke zaman* (Kelantan Through Different Eras) (Kota Bharu: Dian Sdn. Bhd., 1970); Saad Shukri Haji Muda and Abdullah Al-Qari, *Detik-Detik Sejarah Kelantan* (Crucial Moments in Kelantan's History) (Kota Bharu: Penerbit Kelantan, 1971); Rosmera, *Tok Janggut* (Petaling Jaya: Syarikat Buku Uni-text, 1977); Rubaidin Siwar, *Pemberontakan di Pantai Timor* (Rebellion in the East Coast) (Kuala Lumpur: Longman's, 1980); and Haji Buyong Adil, *Perjuangan Orang Melayu Menentang Penjajahan Abad 15–19* (The Malay People's Struggle against Colonialism in the 15th–19th centuries) (Kuala Lumpur: Dewan Bahasa dan Pustaka, 1983).[1]

Contemporary Accounts

I have also consulted the following contemporary accounts and reminiscences about To' Janggut by participants in the British campaign against his rebellion: Carveth Wells, *Six Years in the Malay Jungle* (London: William Heinemann, 1927); W.E. Pepys, "A Malayan Side-Show During World I", *Asiatic Review* 46 (1950): 1174–9; W.E. Pepys, "Kelantan During World War I," *Malaya in History* 6, 1 (1960): 36–9; and the photo albums, papers and journal diaries of A.G. Morkill kept at Rhodes House Memorial Library, Oxford.

Besides these memoirs, I have used the contemporary official correspondence and reports of British military officers, British officials (in Singapore and Kelantan), the Sultan of Kelantan and other local Kelantanese officials who were involved in the affair. These papers are contained in the records of the British Governor/High Commissioner's Office in Singapore, the British Adviser's Office in Kelantan, the Sultan of Kelantan's Palace Office in Kota Bharu, and the Colonial Office in London (in its C.O. 273 and 717 series of correspondence). Copies of these correspondence and reports are available in either the British National Archives in London, the Singapore National Archives in Singapore or in the Malaysian National Archives in Kuala Lumpur.

Scholarly Accounts

Other Malaysian and foreign scholars have done studies on To'

Janggut. Their construction and reconstruction of the To' Janggut story have required me to look at their writings more closely to develop the contours and framework of the To' Janggut story in this book. While I have drawn together some of the materials in their works, I have also tried to assess their relative importance in the historiography of the 1915 Kelantan rebellion.

The earliest study on To' Janggut's rebellion was done by J. de V. Allen, who used mainly the British C.O. records, especially its confidential papers which had then just been opened in London. See his "The Kelantan Rising of 1915: Some Thought on the Concept of Resistance in British Malayan History," published in *Journal of Southeast Asian History* 9 (1968): 241–5. His research was followed by a number of other scholars, which attests to the popularity of the topic: Nik Ibrahim bin Nik Mahmood, who wrote "The To' Janggut Rebellion" (a B.A. honours thesis which was submitted to the History Department at the University of Malaya in 1968), which was subsequently published in a book edited by William R. Roff, *Kelantan: Religion, Society and Politics in a Malay state* (Kuala Lumpur: Oxford University Press, 1974), pp. 62–86. He was followed by Nik Anuar Nik Mahmud's "Sejarah Jeram dan Kebangkitan Tok Janggut," a B.A. honours thesis submitted to the History Department at University of Malaya in 1972, which is still unpublished; Alun Jones' "Internal Security in British Malaya, 1895–1942", a Ph.D. thesis submitted to the History Department at Yale University in 1970, which is still unpublished; and, Khoo Kay Kim, "The Beginnings of Political Extremism in Malaya, 1915–1935", a Ph.D. thesis submitted to the History Department at University of Malaya in 1972, which is still unpublished.

Of these scholars who studied To' Janggut and the 1915 rebellion in the early 1970s, Nik Ibrahim was the first researcher to use Kelantan state administration records, comprising those in the Sultan's Palace Office as well as those in the Kelantan British Adviser's Office. He was also the first to use a local folk source, Yahya Abdullah's *Peperangan To' Janggut, atau Balasan Derhaka* (1955). Nik Anuar Nik Mahmud's 1972 thesis was based mainly on local Kelantanese sources, including interviews with local residents in the Jeram and Pasir Putih districts of Kelantan as well as the works of Kelantanese writers such as Yahya

Abdullah and Saad Shukri Haji Muda. Unlike them, however, Alun Jones followed the tracks of J. de V. Allen by again consulting the British C.O. 273 records and some English-language newspapers published in Singapore such as *The Straits Times*. The period covered by Khoo Kay Kim's thesis is quite close to Alun Jones', and like Alun Jones and J. de V. Allen, his main sources are again the British C.O. 273 records. Alun Jones and Khoo Kay Kim each included a section on the outbreak in Kelantan in their respective thesis. See Alun Jones, pp. 59–71 and Khoo Kay Kim, pp. 76–91.

In 1979 Abdullah Zakaria bin Ghazali, a historian at the University of Malaya, wrote a short essay, "Kebangkitan-Kebangkitan Anti-British Di Semenanjung Tanah Melayu (Anti-British Uprisings in the Malay Peninsula)", in a book, *Malaysia: Sejarah dan Proses Pembangunan* (Malaysia: History and the Process of Development), a collection of essays compiled by the Malaysian Historical Society in Kuala Lumpur (pp. 91–103), in which he examines the 1915 outbreak in four pages. His essay was based mainly on secondary sources, but he did use one local Kelantanese source, Haji Abdullah Amirah's book, *Riwayat Hidup Tok Janggut* (1957). In 1995 University of Malaya historian Shaharil Talib's book, *A History of Kelantan, 1890–1840*, published by the Malaysian Branch of the Royal Asiatic Society, briefly discusses the Kelantan rebellion. He relied heavily on British Kelantan administration and British C.O. records.

In 1999 Abdullah Zakaria bin Ghazali collaborated with two other scholars, Nik Anuar Nik Mahmud and Hanapi Dollah in a book, *Tok Janggut: Pejuang atau Penderhaka?* (Tok Janggut: Freedom Fighter or Anti-Sultan Rebel?), which was compiled and edited by Nik Anuar Nik Mahmud and published by the History Department, Universiti Kebangsaan Malaysia in Bangi. Besides the introduction to the volume, Nik Anuar Nik Mahmud contributed an essay entitled, "Kebangkitan Tok Janggut" (The Tok Janggut Uprising), while Abdullah Zakaria bin Ghazali wrote "Kebangkitan Tok Janggut Dalam Konteks Gerakan Anti-British di Malaysia" (The Tok Janggut Uprising in the context of the Anti-British Movement in Malaysia), and Hanafi Dollah, "Kebangkitan Tok Janggut Dari Perspektif Budaya Politik Melayu Kelantan" (The Tok Janggut Uprising from the Perspective of Kelantanese Political Culture). Their book contains several photographs taken from A.G. Morkill's private album kept at Rhodes House Library in Oxford, U.K. Although Hanafi Dollah in his essay cites Carveth Wells' book, *Six Years in the Malay Jungle*, in which Wells refers to kinship ties between the Sultan and To' Janggut, strangely, this information does not attract the attention of Hanafi Dollah and is hardly discussed in his essay.

Malaysian School History Textbooks

The To' Janggut story is also narrated in Malaysian school history textbooks, which usually follow the brief chronology outlined above. Most, however, have used information taken from local Kelantanese sources. The following selected textbooks all present roughly the same version of the To' Janggut story as it was taught in Malaysian classrooms from the 1960s to the 1990s: Wan Shamsuddin and Arena Wati, *Sejarah Tanah Melayu dan Sekitarnya, 1400–1967* (The History of the Malay Peninsula and surrounding areas, 1400–1967) (Kuala Lumpur: Pustaka Antara, 1969); Joginder Singh Jessy, *Malaysia, Singapura dan Brunai, 1400–1965* (Malaysia, Singapore and Brunei: Longman's, 1975, reprinted 1982 and 1985); and Zainal Abidin bin Abdul Wahid, *et al.*, *Sejarah Tingkatan 2* (Form 2 History; Kuala Lumpur: Dewan Bahasa dan Pustaka, 1991). The last work twice quotes from a local Kelantanese source, *Detik-detik Sejarah Kelantan*, by Saad Shukri Haji Muda and Abdullah Al-qari.

Accounts by Muslim-Malay Authors

Muslim Malay scholars stand out as a group among those who have done research on the rising, but they are divided on how to view it. None of them, however, sees it as a rebellion against the sultan. In an article entitled "The To' Janggut Rebellion of 1915", Ibrahim Nik Mahmood, who researched the topic while a student at University of Malaya, describes the rising as part of an anti-tax movement.[2] Abdullah Zakaria bin Ghazali, a historian at University of Malaya, in articles published in 1979 and 1999,[3] regards it as a nascent anti-British nationalist rising, an explanation also adopted by Islas alias Ariffin Ismail in a university "mini-thesis" analysing the publications of a Kelantanese writer named Yahya Abdullah about the affair.[4] In a study done in 1972, Nik Anuar Nik Mahmud, then a student at the University of Malaya, regarded the rebellion as an anti-tax and anti-British rising, but in 1999 he and Hanapi Dollah, both of them now teaching at Malaysia's National University (Universiti Kebangsaan Malaysia), interpreted the rising as a *Jihad,* or an Islamic holy war, basing their assessment on the timing of the rising in the context of the 1914–9 European war. However, the argument relies on circumstantial evidence, and neither author presents any evidence from the rebel side voicing Islamic sentiments, or support for Turkey. In 1968 James de Vere Allen surmised that there might have been a religious element to the rising because it was led by *penghulus* (village chiefs) and two of the rebel leaders, To' Janggut and Haji Said, were *haji* (men who had gone on the *haj* or pilgrimage to Mecca), but he offered no evidence that To' Janggut had invoked Islamic sentiment, or had sought to fan such feelings in others.[5] Shaharil Talib's 1995 *History of Kelantan, 1890–1940*, discusses the 1915 rebellion in only two pages, and interprets it merely as an attempt by "certain members of the royalty" to reverse the erosion of their traditional powers by the British authorities.

In the Malaysian school history textbook, *Sejarah Tanah Melayu dan Sekitarnya* (1969), both the authors, Wan Shamsuddin and Arena Wati, interpret the rebellion as an anti-British rebellion, although they describe To' Janggut as *alim* (religious). In the history textbook *Sejarah Tingkatan 2* (Secondary 2 History), (1991), Zainal Abidin bin Abdul Wahid, and others, clearly reject the rising as a *perang jihad* (holy war) and view it as an anti-British rebellion. In fact, at the outset, the authors clearly distinguish the difference between the 1915 Kelantan rebellion and the 1928 Terengganu rebellion as follows:

> The rebellions in Kelantan and Terengganu especially worried the British. They feared the rebellion in Kelantan would turn into a holy war. But, in fact, the rebellion in Terengganu more clearly reflected an Islamic character. (The text in Malay reads: Kebangkitan di Kelantan dan Terengganu lebih membimbangkan British. Mereka khuatir kebangkitan di Kelantan menjadi perang jihad. Tetapi, sebenarnya, kebangkitan di Terengganu lebih jelas memperlihatkan unsur Islam.)

The Folk Version

Folk accounts generally present the rebellion as an anti-British rebellion, but those compiled by Yahya Abdullah and Ariffin bin Abdul Rashid especially concentrate in describing the rebellion as *derhaka* or, an act of treason, directed against the ruler as well.[6] Although the Malaysian school history textbooks rely heavily on the folk accounts, they usually follow the official British account that it was both an anti-tax movement and an anti-British uprising. They do not discuss aspects of To' Janggut's defiance of the ruler's authority or examine the sultan's role or involvement. Most of the stories of To' Janggut in children's books adopt a nationalistic view that the uprising was strictly an anti-British rebellion, although they may present variant accounts about To' Janggut's personal background or offer different reasons for his death. None of these accounts view it as a *perang jihad* or holy war.

Official Accounts

Different interpretations of what constituted the true nature of the rising also emanated from the official side. Neither the British authorities nor the Sultan or the Malay administration in Kelantan had viewed the rising as an Islamic *jihad*. Earlier in February, the British administration had crushed the Muslim Sepoy outbreak in Singapore, which involved mainly Muslim Punjabi soldiers from India.[7] As news of the rising spread in Pasir Putih in the first week, the official reports attributed it to political and economic issues at the district level rather than religious issues.

Two Malay plenipoteniaries of the sultan, Dato Menteri (the state secretary) and Dato Bentara Setia (the sultan's secretary), met the British Governor in Singapore on 18 May and reported that "they had not heard the rising was directed against white people", and firmly declared that "it had nothing to do with Turkey being at war with England". They said that based on information they had gathered from villagers in Pasir Putih, the rebellion related only to taxation.[8] British authorities in Kelantan suspected that the people might have strong sympathies for Turkey and for the mutineers in Singapore, and had developed anti-European sentiments as well. W.G. Maxwell, the Colonial Secretary to the Governor who was sent to investigate the causes of the rising, confirmed that such attitudes existed, but he revealed that "unwonted opposition and difficulties [from the Sultan] have been experienced by the British Adviser.... It is not that the Sultan has anything to do with the outbreak."[9] Maxwell's report contained no suggestion that a political Islamic movement lay behind the Kelantan rising. In fact, he flatly asserted, "Opposition to the land-tax was the principal cause of the outbreak."[10]

Interpretations of the To' Janggut Rising
Was the rising directed against the Sultan?

Accounts on the rising by Allen and Nik Ibrahim Mahmood present the Sultan of Kelantan as a pliant pro-British ruler who helped the British authorities suppress the outbreak.[11] Although Allen raises the possibility that the Sultan might be behind the whole rising, he does not investigate the matter further except to state, "It is equally quite possible that the Ruler himself was, by 1915, heartily tired of British rule and prepared to join his relatives in a revolt against it if such a revolt looked like succeeding."[12] The image of a collaborationist sultan also appears in the two folk Kelantanese accounts on the rebellion: *Peperangan To' Janggut atau Balasan Derhaka* (1955) and *Riwayat Hidup To' Janggut dan Peperangnya di Kelantan* (1957). Both accounts depict the peasants as having risen in support of a district feudal lord, Ungku Besar, who opposed new British-imposed land taxes introduced in the name of the sultan, and who wished to re-establish himself in his grandfather's position as a feudal lord. The sultan sends several ministers to the district to negotiate with the rebels, but when they defy his authority he brands them as *penderhaka* (rebels) and seeks British help to suppress them. It is no coincidence that these two folk accounts emphatically call the rebellion *derhaka*, meaning rebellion or "treasonable behaviour" against the sultan. In a study by Tan Ban Teik (1982), oral evidence gathered during field research indicates that some people viewed the rebellion as being against the sultan.[13]

Allen's study, based on Colonial Office records in London, upholds the sultan's version that certain members of the royal family, especially his uncles, were in league with Ungku Besar, the Pasir Putih chief, in a plot to oust him. He argues that they had used the introduction of the new land taxes and peasant dissatisfaction over the conduct of the Pasir Putih district officer, Abdul Latif, as a pretext to launch the rising. The sultan, therefore, was seen as being quite dependent on the British to prop up his throne.

Ibrahim Nik Mahmood, however, rejects the sultan's claim that the rebellion was directed at his own person. Ibrahim argues that the sovereignty of the sultan was merely an "illusion". He asserts that although the Anglo-Kelantan Agreement of 1910 had stated specifically that the ruler had the authority over internal administration, in practice the British Adviser was responsible for the bulk of the laws. He further states as follows:

> ... the rebellion was not, preeminently, a revolt against the sultan — though it is certainly possible that leading rivals for the throne may have been involved after the event — nor yet a nascent state-wide rising.... Rather it was a concerted response to reforms, which, in the eyes of peasants and many of the ruling class alike, constituted an unwarrantable intrusion into their traditional way of life.[14]

Tan Ban Teik, on the contrary, has interpreted the rebellion as directed at the sultan. It was, he says, instigated by To' Janggut for personal reasons, including revenge for the murder of his father by a retainer of the sultan.[15]

Was it an anti-British Adviser rising inspired by the sultan?

Strangely, Allen fails to detect the sultan's antipathy towards the British Adviser throughout the period of the rising. This omission is glaring, since the sultan's criticisms of the B.A.'s role emerge clearly in the reports submitted by the British Adviser, Langham-Carter, and other colonial officials, to the Governor.[16] The difference between an "anti-British" rising and an "anti-British Adviser" rising would be that in the case of the former, the targets were not only the British Adviser but also British nationals, the system of British administration and Britain's role in the European War, while the latter would be specifically directed against the person of the British Adviser and the policies he initiated.

In fact, a difficult relationship had developed between the Sultan of Kelantan and Langham-Carter. W.G. Maxwell, the Colonial Secretary to the Governor who was sent to investigate the causes of the uprising, in his confidential report to the Governor confirmed their strained relationship.[17] While the sultan had been forced to accept British protection, his relationship with individual British Advisers depended on how well their personalities meshed. The sultan did not find Langham-Carter congenial and later had him removed, not an unusual occurrence in the administrative history of British Malaya. Other British Advisers and British Residents in the Malay states encountered similar difficulties. In most official accounts of British Malaya, such conflicts have been played down or concealed, but several instances are brought to light in J.M. Gullick's book, *Rulers and Residents* (1992). Gullick has rightly argued that such conflicts show that the Malay rulers were not always passive puppets dancing to the tune of the Residents or Advisers. They stated their views on many issues but in a quiet way, and often their views were accepted. Gullick presents only a rather abbreviated account of the Kelantan affair, which he describes as "a sad little story of misunderstanding on the part of the *rakyat*, (the people), suspected mischief-making by a disgruntled Malay chief and other aristocrats, and nervous over-action by the British Adviser".[18]

A review of the different versions

Let us consider the interpretation of the first group of scholars, who regard the rising as an anti-British rising. They tend to see the incident, which broke out in Pasir Pasir district, as though it were a Kelantan-wide rising, as well as a nascent nationalist rising. In fact, the outbreak was confined to a remote part of rural Kelantan in Pasir Putih district, although burning of property and minor incidents were reported in the other districts of Pasir Mas and Ulu Kelantan. No British citizen or European was killed. However, it would appear the anti-British sentiment was widespread and the rebels also expressed resentment against non-Kelantanese in general, such as Sikhs and the Singapore-born Malay D.O. of Pasir Putih, Abdul Latif. Other important issues, which require equal attention with the anti-British movement — for instance, the Sultan's ambivalent attitude towards the rising, the folk legend of To' Janggut's disguised pursuit of revenge against the Sultan, and the alleged conspiracy among the Kelantanese aristocrats to oust the

Sultan — suggest that the causes of the rising were more complicated, and need unraveling. The British Adviser, W. Langham-Carter, even denied that the new tax-system was the major cause of the trouble. He attributed the whole plot to efforts originating in Kota Bahru to oust the British over the new land tax that involved both the aristocrats there, whom he labelled "Tungkus", and the Sultan. According to Langham-Carter, however, the aristocrats' ultimate aim was to overthrow the sultan.

The second group of scholars, who argue that the rising was against the Sultan and reflected a combined attempt by both aristocrats and peasantry to oust him because of his acceptance of British protection, however, failed to reckon with the incriminating information which has emerged in British confidential and private sources that rebel leader To' Janggut and the Sultan were related — "cousins of sorts" — and both had secretly been in touch with one another prior to the rising. If the Sultan and To' Janggut were in the plot of the rising, surely a question that needs to be raised is whether the ruler himself might not have been behind the whole thing — if not actively, then at least passively, for fear of his throne: for instance, he had tried to oppose the use of troops. This was a possibility that Allen himself had raised, although he did not pursue the matter much further. While the folk legend reveals nothing of that sort, still it needs to be asked why the British authorities did not expose the ruler's links with To' Janggut or with the aristocrats publicly. This mystery needs to be cleared up.

The third and fourth group of scholars suggests that provincialism was a dominant factor, and that the rising was not only against the land-tax, but was due to Ungku Besar's attempt at secession so that his dynasty could rule Pasir Putih more or less independently of the Sultan at Kota Bahru, the capital. They, too, have failed to link up Ungku Besar's role with the alleged conspiracy of the "Tungkus" in Kota Bharu, the assassination of To' Janggut's father by Ungku Besar's grandfather, the murder of his brother by a henchman of either Ungku Besar's grandfather or the Sultan of Kelantan, and To' Janggut's pursuit of revenge against the latter. Why have all these elements of the To' Janggut story, found only in the folk legend, been ignored by the researchers? These elements I intend to present in the following chapters. Finally, the scholars who argue that the rising was a *jihad*, or the Malay artists of children's story-books who portray To' Janggut as an Islamic radical are merely making a surmise and ignoring the complexity of the issues behind the rising.

Contesting versions: multiple truths

These different scholarly findings reveal that when we uncover and interpret the historical facts, we believe we attempt to reconstruct what the past was really like and, through dint of professional archival research, believe we can get closer to its truthful reality. When we interpret the evidence, we contribute to a presumed centre of "truth" by adding our interpretation to the weight of existing interpretations. The meaning of historical facts so created, in effect, changes as historical interpretations are continually revisited. Thus, each researcher's efforts to achieve validity in his interpretation is constantly undermined or challenged subsequently by some other contradictory evidence, which had not been uncovered by that researcher in his earlier research. It shows that historical reality or truth takes many forms, is always partial, and historically and socially contingent. As British historian Lawrence Stone admitted, in the face of post-modernist attacks on history's basic empiricist principles, "historical truth is unattainable, and that any conclusions are provisional and hypothetical, always liable to be overturned by new data or new theories".[19]

Post-modernists, on the other hand, mock the idea that the human mind mirrors nature and that historians can reflect objectivity. They argue that historical truth or reality is really "multiple", and therefore "unknowable". They argue further that it is impossible for historians ever to achieve historical truth because of their tendency to keep revising their accounts or interpretations of the past "as it actually happened". They are skeptics who have done battle against the nineteenth-century scientific claims that objective truth can be definitively captured. Replying to these arguments, American historians Appleby, Hunt and Jacob in their collaborated study have partially accepted the validity of their argument about how impossible it is to achieve historical truth, when they declared, "Skeptics count this constant reassessing of the past against history's claim to objectivity, whereas it can better be considered testimony to the urgency each generation feels to possess the past in terms meaningful to it. The incontrovertible existence of various interpretations of past events by no means proves the relativist's case, but it certainly demands that everyone shed the positivist's notion of historical truth."[20]

Why has the Kelantan rising attracted so much interest among various scholars? It is probable as Appleby, Hunt and Jacob argue, "Because historical accounts always explain the meaning of events in terms relevant to the immediate audience, curiosity about the past is inextricably bound up in the preoccupations of the present. The past as an object will be read differently from one generation to another." True, and this probably was so in the case of scholars of the Kelantan rising of 1915 who studied it at different times, but the rising also lends itself to being regarded as an example of Malay resistance, in which the key elements of Malay society — the raja, the aristocrats and the peasantry — are all involved.

These elements were found in the Perak and Negri Sembilan rebellions of the 1870s and the Pahang rebellion of the 1890s, as well as in the Kelantan rebellion of 1915, and the Trengganu rebellion of 1925. The first three have been characterised by Allen in his study as falling into the category of "initial resistance", while the remaining two are regarded as examples of "sporadic resistance" (see Allen, "The Kelantan Rising of 1915", *op.cit.*, p. 244). In an essay published in 1988, I argued that these rebellions had failed largely due to lack of Malay unity among the three groups, a point seldom made in the Malay-Muslim scholarly studies of these rebellions.[21] In almost all the rebellions, the Malay rulers initially collaborated with the rebels, but later betrayed and abandoned them in order to reach a compromise with the British colonial power. The rebels received royal encouragement, but increasingly found themselves in an untenable position, as they received royal orders, which seemed confusing and contradictory. Ultimately, as the rulers went over to the British side, the rebels were sacrificed and forced to flee. Many were killed, captured, tried, imprisoned or executed by British troops.

The various Muslim-Malay scholars studying the Kelantan rebellion, while they have been interested in the feudal aspects of traditional Malay society, however, have hardly examined this aspect of the Malay ruler's collaboration and betrayal in the midst of the Malay resistance. Consequently, this perspective has also been carried over into the Malaysian school history textbooks. One explanation for this is that, until 1993, when the Malaysian government amended the Constitution to lift the Malay rulers' immunity from criminal investigation, the Malay-Muslim view was that the sultan's position was sacrosanct, unquestionable. Until 1993, their conduct or any wrongdoing on their part could not come under public scrutiny. Consequently, most Muslim-Malay scholars and writers had tended to adopt a guarded, uncritical, and respectful view of the Malay ruler's role in the anti-colonial struggle. For this reason, those local Kelantanese historians who had presented elements of *lese-majeste* in the 1915 rising and viewed it as *derhaka* to the sultan must constitute an exception. They displayed great courage in recording folk accounts which ran contrary to the official British and Malay versions.

Chapter 3

The Romance of To' Janggut

Although To' Janggut is dead, his story is still remembered by many people and narrated in various versions. Up to the 1970s there were still people who believed that To' Janggut was not dead, and was still in hiding or had disguised his identity.

— S. Othman Kelantan,
novelist and native of Kelantan[1]

"The Romance of To' Janggut" discusses the making and expansion of a folk legend, in which the Kelantanese people, local writers and historians have all played a part. The public infatuation with Tok Janggut's life and adventures keep the stories vibrant and alive in the culture, and they are continually modified and embellished until it becomes difficult to separate myth from reality. In this chapter, several versions of these stories are presented and discussed.

Introduction

The romance of To' Janggut is an integral part of Kelantanese oral folklore, and local writers have recorded folk versions of the story. These accounts differ from those prepared by Malay and British officials and historians. The folk versions provide more colourful details about To' Janggut's life and activities than can be found in the official versions, which are primarily concerned with the political and socio-economic causes of the rebellion. The folk accounts also present To' Janggut's case more sympathetically. Within Kelantanese memories the rebellion is invariably connected with his personality. Thus, the rebellion is called

"Musoh To' Janggut" or "Peperangan To' Janggut", both meaning "To'
Janggut's War".[2] The folk versions also inject an anti-royalty element
into descriptions of the rebellion, describing it as *derhaka*, a word
that means "treason" or "rebellion against the ruler". In fact, the title
of Yahya Abdullah's account is *Peperangan To' Janggut, atau Balasan
Derhaka*, and it deals primarily with To' Janggut's alleged supernatural
powers, his heroism and his defiance of authority.

By injecting an element of anti-royalty or *lese-majeste*[3] into the
legend of To' Janggut, the Kelantanese people have developed a variant
account that challenges the version of the rebellion developed by Malay
ruling authorities. They show their support for To' Janggut's struggle by
regarding him as a hero, and by overtly criticising the Kelantan ruler's
relationships with his subjects, as well as his role and conduct during
the rebellion. The folk legend of To' Janggut can therefore be regarded
as a subversive text. For this reason, its version comprising the elements
of *lese-majeste* has frequently been suppressed. Yet its survival and
persistence within Kelantanese folklore, albeit in a semi-underground
form, demands that it be given proper attention by scholars.

The Folk Legend: Yahya Abdullah's Account

The folk tale or folk legend in Malay literature represents the world-
view of the lower classes. It usually contains elements of farce, satire and
moral judgement, and glorifies magic, the supernatural and superhuman
figures. It has little affinity with the ruling classes. Unlike the stories
of the court-based *hikayat*, which are usually written by palace scribes
and deal mainly with princes and the royal court, folk legends, or folk
hikayat, narrate events and characters found in rural communities. Rulers
are often depicted as clumsy fools, figures of fun who may be symbols
of greed, lust or wickedness. While the court *hikayat* marginalises the
Malay peasant, he comes fully into his own in folk legends.[4] Thus,
when an oral text such as Yahya Abdullah's *Peperangan To' Janggut, atau
Balasan Derhaka* challenges and subverts traditional Malay ideology, we
should be alert to its emphasis, and the way it attempts to give space
and prominence to marginality, in this case to peasant voices and to
peasant characters — in contrast to the court *hikayat* where the dominant
ideology prevails.

Not all versions of the folk legend of To' Janggut have been written down, but the few texts available nevertheless reflect the ingenuity and creativity of the Kelantanese people in constructing their own versions of this historical event. Yahya Abdullah's version is the most important of the folk accounts. In his preface, Yahya describes his sources as follows: "In this little book are narrated one by one in detail the events which occurred as the author has investigated them and which have been recalled from the memories of elderly folks who are knowledgeable in these matters."[5]

The claim that To' Janggut and his father were guilty of *lese-majeste*, as recounted by Yahya Abdullah, does not appear in any of the official British and Malay versions of To' Janggut's rebellion. British interpretations present the rebellion as an anti-British or anti-tax movement, in which the British had the full support of the sultan. By issuing proclamations in the Sultan's name that declared To' Janggut and his supporters to be *penderhaka* or rebels who had risen against his authority, British officials tried to imply that the rebels were also anti-Sultan. They let it be known that the public display of To' Janggut's corpse was done with the Sultan's blessing.

A few British officials were aware of To' Janggut's legend and his cult of invulnerability. This is apparent from a confidential report made by W.G. Maxwell, the Colonial Secretary in Singapore, to the British Governor, in which he said To' Janggut was "not only the leader of the Malays, and the most courageous man amongst them, but also had the reputation of being invulnerable".[6] Another official, W.E. Pepys, the District Officer in Pasir Putih, wrote, "His body was carried to Kota Bahru (for he was reported to be invulnerable, and people in the capital would not have believed a mere report of his death)."[7] Railroad enginer Carveth Wells, who was stationed at Pasir Mas, Kelantan said he had heard that "Tok Janggut had proclaimed himself *kramat* — that is, especially protected by God and invulnerable. To prove it, the old man frequently came out in front of the trenches and allowed the 'army' [British troops] to blaze away at him without effect."[8] If the invulnerability cult has been confirmed, there is, therefore, no reason to dismiss the other folk accounts, especially the anti-royalty aspects, merely on the grounds that the official accounts fail to mention them. Each historical source has its own strengths and weaknesses.

Yahya Abdullah's Original Account

As one of the earliest accounts of the folk legend, Yahya Abdullah's *Peperangan To' Janggut, atau Balasan Derhaka* must be regarded as a daring work for its time. The year of publication (1955) is significant. It was two years before Malaya's independence from British rule. The writer clearly intended to show his nationalistic, if not populist, leanings by recounting the legend of a commoner, glorified by the people of Kelantan. To' Janggut is described as resisting the British government in the cause of social justice and political freedom, defying his own Sultan's authority because of the latter's support of British policies and also in pursuit of personal revenge. Yahya no doubt assumed that the British authorities were unlikely to take action against his version of the folk legend on the eve of Malaya's independence. Since independence occupied people's minds at this time, supporters and members of the Kelantan royal family must also have hesitated to openly attack or reject a work which projected an anti-royalty figure as a nationalist hero or as a freedom fighter against colonial rule, although privately they appeared to have frowned on its publication.

In this account Yahya presents the facts of the rebellion objectively, albeit with great empathy for To' Janggut's cause. Informants recall how they had heard To' Janggut speak about the reasons for his struggle. Yahya's perspective is not avowedly anti-British or anti-Sultan. What is strikingly new is his revelation that To' Janggut was motivated by a desire to seek personal revenge for the death of his father and elder brother at the hand of palace retainers. By implication, this meant that he might have harboured resentment against the Sultan of Kelantan. At the end of his account, Yahya includes a long poem mourning the tragic end of the heroic struggle waged by To' Janggut when his body was left hanging at a public field on the Sultan's orders not far from the Sultan's palace.

Yahya's stories of To' Janggut are deliberately structured to show the social context of the period prior to his rebellion. He describes life in the royal courts before 1915, during a fading feudal period of Kelantan's history when the state came under British rule. He presents folk perceptions of feudal patronage, feudal services and family responsibilities, narrating what happens when patrons and lords fail to look after their subjects, causing subjects to become insubordinate towards their lords in order to defend family honour and responsibilities.

The folk legend portrays To' Janggut as a hero. Born in 1853, he is characterised as a good man who attended a village religious school in his youth, and later went to Mecca to perform the Haj. Because his beard was white, thick and long, reaching down to his chest, he seemed to many people a charismatic figure. Skilled in the martial arts, he was said to possess the powers of invulnerability (*ilmu kebal*). Yahya Abdullah claims that To' Janggut acquired the powers of invulnerability from an immigrant martial arts teacher from Minangkabau.

Yahya's account gives little information about Ungku Besar, or how he came to office.[9] British sources indicate that he was the grandson of Tungku Seri Maharaja, but Yahya Abdullah introduces him by merely stating that Ungku Besar became the feudal lord of Jeram and decided to challenge the new administration in Pasir Putih established by the Sultan of Kelantan.[10] According to Yahya Abdullah, he saw the district officer as usurping his powers and undermining his authority. Under the new rules, land taxes were to be collected from every landowner, including Ungku Besar himself. "It was now decided that regardless of the lineage of the Raja of Jeram, he too was forced to pay all the new taxes, whereas before this he had been exempted."[11] This was humiliating to Ungku Besar, and he began telling people that the new rules were oppressive, and that the district officer, Abdul Latif, a Singapore Malay, was an arrogant and high-handed man. To' Janggut, Penghulu Adam and two other village leaders supported him, and seditious talk spread until it was said that 50 per cent of the Pasir Putih people were on their side. Disturbances and crimes now became rampant in the district, and To' Janggut and other landowners defied the court by refusing to pay taxes. Abdul Latif told several policemen to summon To' Janggut to the district office, and a scuffle broke out, in the course of which To' Janggut stabbed a police sergeant to death. This started the revolt. After the capture of Pasir Putih town by rebel forces, Ungku Besar was declared ruler of Pasir Putih, and To' Janggut his chief minister.

Why did To' Janggut support Ungku Besar's call to resist the new administration? Having earlier narrated the events of *lese-majeste* involving To' Janggut's father, Yahya Abdullah leaves the reader to work out the answer for himself. While To' Janggut's father had tangled with Tungku Seri Maharaja, who was apparently Ungku Besar's grandfather, To' Janggut himself seems to have enjoyed a harmonious relationship with Ungku Besar, who was now acting out of self-interest and had sought the assistance of To' Janggut.

When he discovered that Ungku Besar had lost his powers and office and intended to provoke a confrontation with the Sultan of Kelantan, To' Janggut threw in his lot with him, apparently to seek revenge for his elder brother's death. This seems to be the most logical conclusion for his subsequent conduct. If they succeeded in driving away the district officer, and Ungku Besar returned to rule, he (To' Janggut) would be amply rewarded. By this rationale, To' Janggut seems to have concluded that his father's death had to be accepted, but that of his brother merited retribution.

In their seditious talk to the local people, however, the ringleaders placed greater emphasis on the peasants' alleged dissatisfaction and opposition to the new land taxes than on Ungku Besar's desire to be reinstated to the full powers of his office. In fact, the latter demand was never voiced. In terms of patron-client ties, the ties of obedience and loyalty of To' Janggut towards Ungku Besar, his immediate patron-lord, were naturally closer than his ties with the Sultan of Kelantan, his distant overlord. The former was also closer to the people of Jeram than the latter. The situation demonstrates the feudal nature of Kelantan society. Provincialism favoured the district lord, so that when he decided to take on the state by challenging its district administration, the local people's provincial loyalties were aroused. For Ungku Besar, this was a last chance to wrest back his lost powers. It was a battle for survival, in which he had to take on not only the Sultan of Kelantan, but also the British who supported the Sultan.

Yahya Abdullah's Revised Edition

It is possible that Yahya Abdullah's folk story, *Peperangan To' Janggut, atau Balasan Derhaka*, encountered some opposition from the Kelantan palace. When it was first published by Muslim Printing Press in Kota Bharu in 1955, Yahya Abdullah used a pen name, "Y. Abdullah

Kelantan" (some Kelantanese pronounce his name "Ya-budullah").
Although there is no indication that the book was ever officially banned,
the anti-royalty or *lese-majeste* aspects were deleted in a revised version
of the book published two years later under the title *Riwayat Hidup To'
Janggut dan Peperangan-nya di Kelantan* (The Life of To' Janggut and
His War in Kelantan).

In this revised edition, the name of the compiler (*penyusun*)
is given as Haji Abdullah b. Amirah Seling Kelantan, while the
publisher is Sinaran Brothers of Penang. There is no mention of Yahya
Abdullah's earlier book or of his name on the cover or in the preface,
but the preface reproduces several paragraphs, word for word, from
Yahya Abdullah's original preface while other stories in the book are
identical. The question arises whether the two names, both bearing the
name "Abdullah", refer to one and the same person. In place of the
excised stories dealing with *lese-majeste*, the revised version expands on
To' Janggut's invulnerability cult. The book ends by giving an explicit
account of the public hanging of To' Janggut's corpse in Kota Bharu,
the Kelantan capital, as recalled by several informants.

The revised version of Yahya Abdullah's account of the folk legend
omits the first 17 pages of the earlier book, which contain the episodes
of *lese-majeste* involving Tungku Seri Maharaja. Instead, it provides
additional information regarding To' Janggut's personal background,
focusing on how he acquired his powers of invulnerability and his
propensity for violence. This description of the negative side of To'
Janggut's personality cult is more balanced than Yahya Abdullah's
previous account. The narrator then introduces "Ungku Besar Tuan
Ahmad ibnu Al-Marhum Engku Chik Pendek", who is described as
the ruler of Jeram who had for long enjoyed the respect and loyalty of
the local people but who had lately felt that their feelings for him had
declined because the new district officer had undermined his status.

The revised version nevertheless extols To' Janggut's exploits and
regards him as a famous figure. It begins by stating that To' Janggut
was born in 1850, three years earlier than the year recorded in Yahya
Abdullah's previous account. It says that after the birth, the midwife
told his mother to dry his umbilical cord and keep it for the occasion of
his circumcision. If she then mixed it in rice porridge and fed it to her

son, he would become strong and invulnerable. When he was between three and four, he was already quite wild and uncontrollable. Though he was bitten by dogs and gored by horned animals, he was not badly hurt. At seven, he was already a recalcitrant, but showed a courageous streak. In any wrestling match or sword fight with other children, he was a bad loser. At 18, when he was circumcised, his father fed him his own umbilical cord as directed. By the age of 25 he had acquired a reputation in his village as a fearless fighter and leader of his own gang of men, who patrolled the village at night to protect the residents against robbers. When a thief was caught, To' Janggut meted out a beating or executed the criminal. His character included a mean streak. He was a bad loser in gambling. He indulged in bullfights and cockfights, and was known to have lost his temper once and knifed a man to death. By the time he was 28, but before he left for Mecca, he was said to have killed eight men. He was also known to have two wives. Because of his long, white beard, all strata of Malay society in Kelantan knew Mat Hassan bin Monas, or Haji Mat Hassan, as To' Janggut.[12]

The Kelantanese appear to have been proud of To' Janggut's reputation as a Kelantanese who was courageous, a devout Muslim, a good fighter, and had an aura of invulnerability.[13] The following stanza from Yahya Abdullah's long poem captures well the provincial sentiments of the Kelantanese:

> *To' Janggut anak Kelantan*
> *Tempat beranak Kampung Jeram*
> *Handal berani bukan buatan*
> *Mimpian rakyat dengan tenteram.*

> To' Janggut a native of Kelantan
> Was born in Kampung Jeram
> His fighting courage was no mere fiction
> It fired the people's imagination.[14]

In the final moments of the skirmish with the British armed forces, To' Janggut, despite his alleged invulnerability, fell to a foe who was said to be "shrewder, more skilful and invincible". According to both versions of the folk legend, men, women and children wept when To' Janggut's corpse was carried around the town of Kota Bahru in a bullock-cart on the orders of the Sultan of Kelantan. The exhibition or "show" passed through every street and corner of the town in order to show the people "the punishment meted out for rebellion against the ruler and the state".[15]

Other Versions of the Folk Legend

Ariffin bin Abdul Rashid's Account

In 1960, three years after the publication of the revised edition, another attempt was made to retell the folk legend, including the parts dealing with *lese-majeste*, by Kelantanese writer Ariffin bin Abdul Rashid, in a book entitled *Peristiwa-Peristiwa Di Kelantan* (Events in Kelantan).[16] He presented what appears to be a different version of the folk legend, one that leaves out references to the Sultan of Kelantan in connection with the murder of To' Janggut's eldest brother, Mat Tahir. Ariffin explains the death as follows: "When Monas' son Mat Tahir, that is, To' Janggut's elder brother, was killed by a *budak raja* although he (the son) committed no wrong, and the raja did not heed his request for justice and revenge against the murderer, then anger arose in his (Monas') heart towards the raja and he waited for the opportunity to show his displeasure."[17] In Malay the construction of this sentence is vague and it is not clear whose "*budak raja*" killed Mat Tahir. It could imply that the ruler involved in that murder was Seri Maharaja Jeram, the feudal chief of Jeram district, against whom his father, Panglima Monas, decided to commit *lese-majeste*. For this crime, Monas was murdered by a strongman of Seri Maharaja Jeram, Pa' Sulong Bulat. Ariffin seems to suggest that To' Janggut's elder brother, Mat Tahir, had been murdered by Tungku Seri Maharaja's slave. If a reader had not seen Yahya Abdullah's account, Ariffin's version would seem to imply that it was the *budak raja* of Seri Maharaja Jeram who had murdered both members of To' Janggut's family, first, his elder brother and then his father. Ariffin clearly states that revenge became the motivation for To' Janggut's mission after he returned from Mecca and discovered the truth behind the murders, news of which had reached him in Mecca. "On his arrival in kampung Jeram, he learnt the truth of these rumours. Then in his heart arose the desire to seek revenge for his father's death."[18]

One puzzling question is this: by leaving out the Sultan of Kelantan's role in the murder of his brother, has Ariffin deliberately modified or distorted the folk legend? Moreover, Ariffin's account omits the name of Ungku Besar Jeram, the successor of Seri Maharaja Jeram, in connection with To' Janggut's rebellion. In the folk legend, as well as in all official British and Malay palace accounts, Ungku Besar is known as To' Janggut's patron and lord. The police and military authorities identified both men as ringleaders of the rebellion, and announced rewards for their arrest, but Ariffin does not mention Ungku Besar at all. By omitting Ungku Besar, he gives the impression that To' Janggut's struggle was actually aimed at Seri Maharaja Jeram, although by this time he was already dead, or at least had vacated the Jeram throne. When To' Janggut and his men seized the district administration of Pasir Putih, the Sultan of Kelantan is suddenly brought into the story. Ariffin says he was angry with To' Janggut (*Sultan Muhammad murka kepadanya*, p. 46) and issued instructions to crush the rebellion. Thus, in Ariffin's version, Seri Maharaja Jeram does not appear to have died at the time of the rising, while in Yahya Abdullah's account of the folk legend Ungku Besar Jeram has succeeded him in office. Ariffin's version would not have been credible to older Kelantanese who knew that Ungku Besar had joined To' Janggut in the rebellion. Ariffin also describes how the corpse was brought to Kota Bharu by Indian troops and the ceremony ordered by the Sultan of Kelantan to show it around the town, so that the public could see "the retribution for one who had risen against the ruler and the state", and then bring it to Padang Bank, in front of "Istana Sultan" (the Sultan's Palace), and suspend it for an hour, legs up and head down, to be seen by "thousands of people from far and near". Ariffin says, "Up till now, people still visit his grave as a shrine and revere him." He concludes his version of the story by penning a pantun (a four-line stanza) to remember the heroic deeds of To' Janggut as a true son of Kelantan (*untuk mengenangkan kehandalan penglima To' Janggut anak Kelantan yang sejati*).

> *Asal To' Janggut orang Kelantan*
> *Gagah berani seperti syaitan*
> *Mati berperang untuk kebebasan*
> *Kuburnya terletak di Pasir Pekan.*

To' Janggut a true Kelantanese was he
Fearless like the devil
He died fighting for freedom
And lies buried in Pasir Pekan.[19]

Sa'ad Shukri Haji Muda's Account

Another account that illustrates the anxiety which Kelantanese writers face when writing about To' Janggut's rebellion was composed by local historian Sa'ad Shukri Haji Muda. In his *Sejarah Kelantan* [History of Kelantan], published in 1962, Sa'ad Shukri, the brother of a former Mentri Besar or Chief Minister of Kelantan, Datuk Mohd Asri bin Haji Muda, preferred to frame the account he presents of the rebellion as that of an elderly informant of royal background. The informant begins by offering felicitations to the Sultan of Kelantan, and by utilising the term *ayahanda* (father) in his greeting, which implies that he was a member of the Kelantan royalty.[20] Perhaps because of his direct or indirect relationship with the Sultan, this narrator avoids many of the details found in other local accounts, including the events of *lese-majeste* found in Yahya Abdullah's and Ariffin's versions. This narrative follows the officially sanctioned version, repeating that the rebellion was aimed at new taxes on land and crops, that To' Janggut himself refused to pay taxes, that he murdered a police sergeant, and that the Sultan of Kelantan asked for British troops to put down the rebellion. To' Janggut is not treated as a hero. The narrative concludes with the revelation that To' Janggut's corpse was exhibited in two different places, a detail that departs from the description of the treatment of the corpse in the accounts by Yahya Abdullah and Ariffin bin Abdul Rashid. This version states that the corpse was first brought to Padang Bank in front of the Sultan's place in Kota Bahru and propped up on a wooden post for the public to view, and then taken to the village of Pasir Pekan where it was crucified upside down, legs up and head down (*songsang* in Malay) for three days and three nights, and then taken down to be buried.

Revised Version of Sa'ad Shukri Haji Muda's Book by Abdullah Al-qari bin Haji Salleh

In 1971 Abdullah Al-qari bin Haji Salleh released a revised edition of

Sa'ad Shukri Haji Muda's appeared book, entitled *Detik-Detik Sejarah Kelantan* (Crucial Moments in Kelantan's History). The revision adopts a nationalistic perspective and presents To' Janggut's struggle in a more favourable light than in the earlier edition. It calls the uprising *Musoh To' Janggut* (To' Janggut's War), repeating the phrasing that had been used in most popular versions of this story, but it still leaves out the events of *lese-majeste* associated with To' Janggut's father's death, or his disguised pursuit of revenge, found in Ariffin bin Abdul Rashid's and Yahya Abdullah's accounts. This revised version of Muda's book contains additional information about the events following the capture of Pasir Putih town by rebel forces. Ungku Besar, it says, was appointed "sovereign ruler", To' Janggut chief minister, Haji Sa'id his deputy, and Encik Ishak the new district chief. It reveals that To' Janggut and his men put up a "brave" fight, but adds, "unfortunately To' Janggut suffered defeat, indeed he was killed and his followers fled to Siam, Mat Kelantan (also known as Mat Saman, one of his followers) was given a prison sentence of eight years, but after several months he was released". On the failure of To' Janggut's invulnerability, it says: "To' Janggut, who was invulnerable and whose body could not be pierced by bullet, finally met his death at the sharp end of a colonialist's bayonet." This, however, is at variance with other local accounts, and also with those of British officials who were involved in the skirmish, which all state that To' Janggut died from bullet wounds. On the public hanging of his corpse, it describes the viewing public as being "in a state of nervousness" (*orang ramai yang sedang di dalam kebimbangan itu*), and that the display was done "as a form of humiliation by the colonial authorities".[21]

Mohd. Hashim Khalin bin Haji Awang's Account

In 1970, another Kelantanese writer, Mohd. Hashim Khalin bin Haji Awang followed Sa'ad Shukri Haji Muda in retelling the story of To' Janggut, again without mentioning the murder of To' Janggut's brother or the elements of *lese majeste* connected with his father's death in his book, *Kelantan dari zaman ke zaman* (Kelantan through different eras). The author explains that the uprising was due to the refusal of the villagers of Pasir Putih and To' Janggut to pay taxes, that To' Janggut killed the police sergeant who attempted to handcuff him, and that after he was killed, To' Janggut's corpse was hanged, "upside down for three days" at Padang Bank in Kota Bharu for the public to view. "After this incident," says the author, "the state of Kelantan returned to peace and prosperity."[22]

Scholarly Use of Local Folk Legends

Three university-based scholars, Ibrahim Nik Mahmood and Nik Anuar Nik Mahmud,[23] and Islas alias Ariffin bin Ismail[24] cite Yahya Abdullah's and Ariffin's work in the bibliographies of their studies of the rebellion. Their studies were completed respectively in 1971 and 1972 at the University of Malaya, and in 1984 at Science University of Malaysia. None of them, however, mentions the legend or makes any reference to *lese-majeste*. All use details of To' Janggut's personal life drawn from Yahya Abdullah's account and the revised version, *Riwayat Hidup To' Janggut*, to flesh out their biographical accounts of him. It is possible that their reluctance to use these aspects of the story might have stemmed from an inability to "prove" the historicity of the local stories. But local histories, suggesting possibilities of plurality and difference, as shown by Lorraine M. Gesick in the case of Lady White Blood, a southern Thai legend, could be presented as a local historical discourse that exists outside of the royal capital, in a remote district, and is multi-vocal, with more than one version of a story understood as being "true", depending on locale.[25]

Tan Ban Teik's study, completed at Universiti Sains Malaysia in 1982, uses an abbreviated form of the folk legend.[26] Tan draws on an oral source (a Kelantan informant), and on Ariffin bin Abdul Rashid's 1960 book, *Peristiwa-peristiwa di Kelantan*. The version of the folk legend given by his informant states that one of the Sultan of Kelantan's sons killed To' Janggut's eldest brother, and because the Sultan did not investigate or take action against his son, Panglima Monas committed *lese-majeste* by having an affair with one of the Sultan's concubines, Wan Serang Bulan. This differs from Yahya Abdullah's and Ariffin's accounts: the former identifies the killer of To' Janggut's older brother as a follower of the Sultan, and the latter claims that the brother's killer was a slave of Tengku Seri Maharaja.

According to Tan's version, the murder of his father caused To' Janggut to seek vengeance against the Sultan of Kelantan. The storyline in Yahya's account implies that To' Janggut's rebellion was, in fact, aimed at the Sultan of Kelantan. Tan's version blends his oral source and Ariffin's account, as the following passage from his study clearly shows: "To' Janggut's father, Monas, became angry and hence wanted to defy the Sultan. He had an affair with one of the Sultan's concubines named Wan Serang Bulan. This was later discovered by the Sultan. As a result, Monas was killed by the Sultan's man and Wan Serang Bulan was sent into exile. At that time To' Janggut was on a pilgrimage to Mecca. Hearing the news that his father was dead, To' Janggut hurried back to Kelantan in 1907 to find out what caused his father's death. In the end, he knew the truth. Then the urge to seek revenge for the murder of his father rose in his heart. "Maka naiklah dendam dihatinya hendak menuntut bela di atas kematian bapanya itu."

The Malay quotation in the last line is taken from Ariffin's book. However, although he read Ariffin's version, Tan appears to have been persuaded by his informant's account that it was the son of the Sultan of Kelantan who had murdered To' Janggut's brother. In Tan's version, the two individuals who figure in Yahya Abdullah's version of *lese-majeste*, Seri Maharaja Jeram and the Sultan of Kelantan known as "Mulut Merah", have become a single person, the Sultan of Kelantan who ruled in 1915. However, by quoting the last line from Ariffin's account, which Ariffin attributes to Tungku Seri Maharaja, Tan has juxtaposed it in such a way that it relates to the Sultan of Kelantan. One possible explanation for his reading of Ariffin's account is the vagueness with which the author couched his text, especially his use of the word "raja" in a context that leaves the identity of the "raja" unclear.

S. Othman Kelantan and the Folk Legend

In 1980, a novel about To' Janggut by a well-known Kelantanese novelist, S. Othman Kelantan, was published.[27] The novel *Perwira* [Hero] narrates the fictional exploits of Awang Teleng, one of To' Janggut's followers, who after his leader's death continues his struggle against the British administration until he himself is captured and killed by British troops. In a paper presented to a seminar on To' Janggut in Kota Bharu in 1996, S. Othman Kelantan recounted his unhappy experiences in relation to the folk legend. He hinted that the Kelantan palace, if not local Malay officials, had always been uneasy about the folk legend of To' Janggut. This became clear in 1970, he said, when a 96-year-old man appeared in Kuantan and declared that he was a freedom fighter, warrior and fugitive named Mat Kelantan who had been involved in To' Janggut's struggle. The man was promptly denounced as a fraud by the palace, which said the public should not believe the story.[28] In his seminar paper, S. Othman Kelantan explained why an early draft of his novel entitled "To' Janggut", which he completed in 1957 based on Yahya Abdullah's 1955 life of To' Janggut, was never published, and why 25 years later he decided to write the novel *Perwira* about a follower of To' Janggut instead of about the famous folk hero himself. S. Othman Kelantan recalled,

I already had a hunch that my novel *To' Janggut* could never be published in Malaysia. This is not due to its contents as a novel of creative imagination but because of the To' Janggut story itself. This is borne out by what had happened to my earlier work, a play entitled *Awang Teleng*, which I had written at the request of a friend. This drama reconstructed the historical atmosphere of To' Janggut in the context of a courageous Awang Teleng. It was scheduled to be staged in Kuala Krai. Tickets had been sold and the public response was good. Suddenly, however, the sponsors informed me that the police authorities had refused permission for it to be staged. The reason was that the director had written a synopsis mentioning the history of To' Janggut in the programme and in the script of Awang Teleng.

I had deliberately not referred to the story of To' Janggut because I knew the situation in Kelantan would not allow it. It was for this reason that I had created instead the character of Awang Teleng and other-fighters who were involved in To' Janggut's rebellion. The others included Haji Said Merbol, Encik Ishak, Hussain Harimau, Abas Berani, Abdul Rahman Anak Kerbau, Ali Kebal, Penghulu Adam, Haji Senik Gong Datuk and Mat Saman. These are real names in history of people who were involved directly in To' Janggut's rebellion.

If they had been presented as real historical figures together with To' Janggut, it is certain it would raise unpleasant implications.

Because of that I created the fictitious character of Awang Teleng, who together with his comrades defended Kelantan from foreign rule, but set against the historical background of To' Janggut. This was to reconstruct the atmosphere of To' Janggut clearly, but not the figure of To' Janggut as a historical figure directly. What I referred to was only the period in passing before and after 1915.[29]

Based on historical details in Yahya Abdullah's book and the oral accounts of older people, including his elderly aunt, S. Othman Kelantan had intended to expand further the historical development of To' Janggut's story. "The reason is that although To' Janggut is dead, his story is still remembered by many people and narrated in various versions. Up to the 1970s there were still people who believed that To' Janggut was not dead, and was still in hiding or had disguised his identity. And, moreover, there were other stories related to his struggle about events involving other people...."[30] "Because To' Janggut is well known in history and his rebellion occurred recently in 1915, it is difficult for the imagination to reconstruct his character. To' Janggut is a real-life personality but has been transformed into a legend, a figure who has been raised to a high pedestal, hero-worshipped and remembered for his heroism in fighting against the British. He had a large following. And to perpetuate his memory I've narrated the stories of his followers."[31]

Conclusion

To' Janggut's rebellion entered popular consciousness as an event by which to measure time or to fix a date. Recalling the impact of this single event in the people's perceptions, W.E. Pepys recalled: "It added a new date to the chronology of the Raiat [the people] of the Pasir Puteh District. Hitherto they had dated every event in their lives by the 'Great Wind' which about 1880 swept over the Kelantan plain and denuded it of all timber. Thus they would say, 'At the time of the Great Wind I was so high' or 'My son was not yet born' and so on; but from now onwards they said, 'At the time of To' Janggut I was so and so'."[32]

Chapter 4

To' Janggut's War, or
the Retribution for Rebellion

> His body was taken to the capital...
> Hung legs up and head down
> Crowds watched this spectacle
> As if the corpse was being roasted
> For an hour it was exposed.
> — Poem by Yahya Abdullah

This chapter contains my translation of the folk version of the story of To' Janggut's rebellion as related by Yahya Abdullah (also known as Y'Abdullah Kelantan) in his *Peperangan To' Janggut, atau Balasan Derhaka* (To' Janggut's War, or the Retribution for Rebellion), a work first published in the Malay Jawi script in 1955 by the Muslim Printing Press in Kota Bahru, Kelantan, and subsequently reissued under the title, *Riwayat Hidup To' Janggut dan Peperangannya di Kelantan* (1957). Little is known about this author except that he was born in Kampung Banggol, near Kota Bahru, was educated at the Sultan Idris Teachers' College at Tanjong Malim in Perak, and returned to teach at a Malay school in Kelantan. He retired on health grounds in 1964 and died in 1969.[1]

I present the translation of this local folk legend here in order to let it stand on its own. In this way, I do not privilege any one version over another. Each version of the 1915 rebellion has its own criteria for historical "truth" and historical "proof" informed by that historical sensibility. This is a version of how the Kelantanese people in Pasir Putih district view the 1915 rebellion. It is presented as To' Janggut's personal war. Let me recapitulate briefly with some comments below:

The folk story begins with To' Janggut's father, Panglima Monas, who commits *lese-majeste* or, *derhaka*, with the seduction and rape of Wan Serang Bulan, his lord's concubine. This was done to "ruin his lord's life" because the lord had ignored his appeal for assistance to avenge the murder of his son, Mat Tahir [To' Janggut's brother], by a retainer of the Sultan of Kelantan. Monas is later executed. At the time of Monas' death, To' Janggut is in Mecca. The folk version narrates the rising in terms of To' Janggut's disguised pursuit of revenge, his leadership and how he came to be drawn in with Ungku Besar's plan to boost his fading feudal powers and the peasants' dissatisfaction over the new land taxes.

The story can be read as a morality or fairy tale (the beautiful concubine seduced, and the dire consequences that follow). It is also an adventure yarn about an irascible, quixotic, swash-buckling hero, who defies great odds. The story is one of a conflict between tradition and change, and between resistance and authority. Within this framework the folk narrative invents or reinvents its own motif, values and imagery. Where the official narrative sees To' Janggut merely as an anti-tax rebel, the folk version presents him as a heroic, invulnerable figure, fighting for social justice. Like his father, he defies the feudal authority. The folk text is, therefore, a subtle critique of Malay feudal society and its values. To' Janggut's unexpected stabbing of a police sergeant, who was acting under instructions from a British-appointed District Officer, makes him accidentally responsible for starting the rebellion. He further defies the Sultan's orders that he call off the rebellion and surrender. The narrative becomes intricate, ironic, and suggests even more than it appears: making To' Janggut achieve what he most wants and to be what he says he is not. A long poem on the public hanging of his corpse — the Sultan's "retribution" for "To' Janggut's fight for freedom" — closes the narration.

[Below is the translated text of Yahya Abdullah's *Peperangan To' Janggut, atau Balasan Derhaka*.][2]

Before readers are introduced to To' Janggut, it may be proper to sketch the background of the administration of Kelantan under various Malay rulers before the state came under British influence.

In the mid-eighteenth century (circa 1756) Long Ghaffar (Jaafar) ruled Kota Jeram. He was a relative of Long Yunus, the ruler of Kelantan. He was conferred a very full range of powers in Jeram short of taking a life, for which he had to obtain the approval of the ruler who resides in Kota Bharu. His territory of Jeram extended from the Sungei Pasir Tumbuh to the south until the border with Trengganu at Pacakan.

According to the story of how Pacakan got its name, His Highness Long Yunus and his cousin Long Jaafar had just returned from a game of cock-fighting with a Bugis Panglima in Trengganu. After winning the game, the ruler of Trengganu commanded his chiefs to escort the two Kelantanese princes to Kelantan. It had been with the princes' help that the kingdom of Trengganu had been able to escape the clutches of the Bugis Rajas who aspired to conquer Trengganu.

The royal escorts were told that wherever the two princes intended to set up an administration, there the escorts were to plant stakes to demarcate the areas of their rule. And so after the two princes and their royal escorts had moved up from the Trengganu coastline into Kelantan, they reached a place close to Kampung Semerak (Cerang Ruku).

His Highness Long Yunus planted his walking stick into the ground to indicate that he intended to be ruler of the eastern territory of Kelantan. Whereupon the escorts returned to Trengganu and conveyed his intention to the ruler of Trengganu. It was for this reason that henceforth the place was called Pacakan (the planting of the stake).

In addition, to the west and north of Sungai Pasir Tumbuh up to the Bukit Tanjung (within the territory of Thailand today), all the territory was also within the jurisdiction of Sultan Long Yunus.

As for His Highness Long Ghaffar, he established his fortification and palace at Jeram in the year 1756. He governed on behalf of Sultan Long Yunus who lived in Kota Bharu. So did his descendants up to 1878 when the office fell to His Highness Tungku Seri Maharaja Tua.

Kota Jeram (Jeram Fort) was situated three and a half miles southeast from the town of Pasir Putih. Within its confines Kota Jeram contained nine neat, comfortable and solid wooden houses. Kota Jeram stood on the bank of a stream whose clear waters came from the Jeram River.

The existence of the stream added to the beauty of Kota Jeram. Around the fort ran a moat which was dug to hinder an enemy from easily capturing it. At the entrance of the fort stood several small cannons and cannonballs.

While His Highness Seri Maharaja Tua ruled in Kota Jeram, he held office as the governor who was responsible to Sultan Raja Tuan Senik Mulut Merah (Sultan Senik the Sultan with the red mouth), who was from the lineage of Sultan Long Yunus.

Like most governors, he was provided with several retainers and slaves. One of his trusted bodyguards was Monas. Wherever he went Tengku Seri Maharaja Tua took him along with him.

Monas had two sons, Mat Tahir and Mat Hassan. The older son died while he was a young man, while trading at Padang Garung near Kota Bharu. He was killed by a retainer (*budak raja*) of His Royal Highness Sultan Tuan Senik Mulut Merah (Sultan with the red mouth). The retainer was said to have committed the murder without fear of being challenged or questioned.

The younger son, Mat Hassan, was born in 1853 in Jeram. As a boy, he learnt the Quran under a *lebai*, a person noted for his religious piety. He later attended a religious school (*madrasah*). He was also trained in martial arts by an elderly immigrant Minangkabau who was said to be an invincible fighter.

Not long after he studied at the madrasah, Mat Hassan made a pilgrimage to Mecca to fuilfil one of the five obligations of Islam. He stayed on in Mecca for several years to acquire religious knowledge and then returned to Jeram to find his father Monas had been murdered by Pak Sulung Bulat, a henchman of Tungku Seri Maharaja Tua Jeram.

The reason for the murder was related to the death of his elder brother Mat Tahir, as narrated earlier. When Monas learnt of the circumstances of his son's death by the Sultan's *budak raja*, he had appealed to his master, the Raja of Jeram (Tungku Seri Maharaja Tua), for help.

But his lord treated his plea lightly. He did not even show a hint of interest, let alone sympathy. Whereupon overcome with anger the idea entered his mind to ruin his master's life. Thereafter, relations between them became bad.

Months passed. Then one day Tungku Seri Maharaja Tua decided to pass his time at Semerak. He planned to leave with a retinue of officials and escorts including Pak Sulung Bulat his second bodyguard. He summoned Monas and ordered him to look after the palace while he was gone for a few days.

"Are you bringing along your Royal Consort and mistresses with you?" asked Monas.

"My journey is a secret even to them, for you know how it is, when these women are informed, they all will want to come, too, so please do not tell them."

Monas promised.

Next morning the ruler left, offering Monas the opportunity that he had been waiting for. He lost no time in ensuring that the ruler would be separated from the concubine whom he loved very much, Wan Serang Bulan.

The lady was an extremely attractive woman, with a slim waist, light tan skin, long and smooth hair that reached her shoulder, and the smiles from her red lips were like emeralds and would befuddle the mind of any beholder. Her tight and slim waist suggested that she was not sexually satisfied.

At the village of Saring towards the south, there was a public performance of the Mak Yong, a popular Kelantanese dance show. On the second day of the show, Panglima Monas went to the palace and lied to Wan Serang Bulan, saying that Tungku Seri Maharaja had asked for her to meet him there — because a wicked idea had developed in his head.

On hearing this, Wan Serang Bulan went to her room to change into pretty clothes and to apply some perfumes to make herself presentable to her lord. Then she left the palace with Panglima Monas.

As it transpired, her expectations did not materialize because the person in whom she put her trust now betrayed her. After they had gone on more than half the way, Monas took her against her will. In committing this despicable act, he had defied his religion. He knew that he could never escape punishment.

By chance they were seen by one of the palace women as they returned, and she asked Wan Serang Bulan, "Well, well, what's our lady doing, enjoying herself at night and in the morning, in the absence of our lord?"

The seduction of Wan Serang Bulan by Monas

[Illustration taken from Yahya Abdullah, *Peperangan To' Janggut, atau Balasan Derhaka* (1955)]

Wan Serang Bulan was shocked. She began to tremble. Soon she revealed what Monas had done to her. With tears in her eyes, she begged her friend, "Cik Suri, please do not threaten me, but protect me by concealing the secret of the incident with Monas, otherwise if it gets out, Maharaja Tua will certainly kill me."

Cik Suri demanded the full details of the incident, otherwise His Highness would be told of it.

Her mind disturbed by her friend's threat, whether she wished it or not, Wan Serang Bulan began narrating to her the incident, as she wiped away tears from her eyes. Then she begged her friend again to keep the secret.

However, two or three other concubines appeared. Soon they, too, learned about the incident. You could cork the mouth of a bottle but not the mouths of these women!

And they each remarked that it was unlikely anything would happen to the most favourite concubine of His Highness. Each of them pursed her lips as she returned to her room.

Wan Serang Bulan entered her room and flung herself on the bed, overcome with fear and sadness. It is impossible for this writer to convey how depressed she was. This member of the gentle sex was unable to stop crying as she dreaded the punishment of His Highness.

The following day Raja Jeram returned. This increased her anxiety and soon her fears were justified. His Highness, on discovering the incident, without hesitation ordered his bodyguard Pak Sulong Bulat to execute Panglima Monas for the crime he had committed and for betraying his lord's trust in him.

Wan Serang Bulan was expelled from the palace and prohibited from living in Jeram.

Panglima Monas was killed by Pak Sulung Bulat in Cenderung Tok Sening in Pengkalan Sungai Jeram. He thrust a metal lance into the neck of Panglima Monas as the latter bent down to scoop up some water to wash his face before prayers.

His body was buried on the spot where he fell. It is where the Jeram Malay School now stands. Thus, ended the life of Monas, the father of Haji Hassan who had just returned from Mecca.

The nickname of Haji Hassan was To' Janggut. He had grown his beard long and thick down to his chest after his return from Mecca, and had become a conspicuous figure. He was six feet tall. His body was lean and slightly dark, his eyes round and piercing, indicating cunning and shrewdness.

His chin was square, his head large and his crown bald. His eye-brows were bushy, which indicated a firm and determined mind. In short, he was an impressive figure. He liked to wear a green shirt and a green head-cloth. Tucked into the waist of his sarong was a kris with nine curves, worn Minangkabau-style.

He was a kind man who was always willing to assist anyone in hardship, regardless of race. However, he hated any oppressor. He once stabbed and killed a man who was cruel to another.

To' Janggut was extremely fond of breeding animals for sport and competitions, such as bulls, goats and cockerels. He was also a businessman who traded in rice, padi and coconut oils. His wife and children helped him in the business. He often travelled on business to Trengganu and Patani.

In Jeram he was known to have assisted in the digging of irrigation canals to facilitate the flow of the Rasau River to the rice fields in Pasir Putih, especially at Kampung Kelubi.

Now let me relate how the rebellion of To' Janggut came about and resulted in armed clashes with the Government forces.

Pak Sulung Bulat thrusts his lance into the neck of Panglima Monas

[Illustration taken from Yahya Abdullah, *Peperangan To' Janggut, atau Balasan Derhaka* (1955)]

The opening up of Pasir Putih

Although Pasir Putih is now the fourth district[3] of Kelantan, it was formerly a forested area especially along the coast between Pasir Putih and Semerak. Between 1800 and 1900 Pasir Putih was known as Pengkalan Limbungan because it was a place for making large boats and sailing perahus. Hence, the name *limbungan* (dock).

The boat-builders were skilled craftsmen, whose reputation was as good as if not better than those in Trengganu. Pengkalan Limbungan had a deep harbour for the constructed boats to be lowered in.

Pengkalan Limbungan did not have more than 1,000 people. Their favourite past-times were gambling at bull-fights, cock-rights or fish-fights (using the fighting fish *sepilai*) and other sports.

Consequently, quarrels and clashes broke out frequently among the spectators who came from various villages and led to bloodshed.

One day there was a major brawl between Mat Saman Limbungan and Haji Encik Long from Kamunting, over the high stakes they had betted. There was nothing the village chief could do to stop it.

News of this reached the ears of the Sultan of Kelantan, Tungku Long Senik, or better known as Sultan Muhammad IV.

The authority of Kota Bharu about 1911

The Kelantan ruler paid a visit to Pengkalan Limbungan, accompanied by a string of state officials including the Raja of Jeram, Tun Ahmad Ibn Almarhum Ungku Cik Pandak, and To' Janggut.

After the rival groups were brought together, peace was restored and the ruler returned to the capital, not before appointing Penghulu Dollah to take charge of the district. He was ordered to set up a police station and a courthouse.

Penghulu Dollah found suitable sites for these buildings. When they were completed, the Sultan returned to the town for its official launch with several chiefs and a man who was a native of Singapore named Encik Yen.

The official launch of Limbungan as a district was marked by pomp and pageantry. The cannons fired a royal salute. The people roared with pleasure as the ruler declared open a new bull-ring. The bulls were led into the ring for a contest. The celebrations lasted seven days and seven nights.

On the seventh day, the Sultan proclaimed that from henceforth, the town would no longer be known as Limbungan but would be called Pasir Putih (white sands) because of the white sands all around it. The population cried out in support of the decision.

The ruler further announced the appointment of Encik Yen from Singapore as the first District Officer of Pasir Putih. Later, several village heads were appointed as well as policemen to staff the police station under Sergeant Sulaiman.

Then the ruler returned to the capital. The day-to-day administration of Pasir Putih district came to take effect. The district's population increased, with many people clearing the jungle for the cultivation of crops and the construction of the town's offices. As the new village heads were instructed in their responsibilities, Pasir Putih town became peaceful and prosperous.

To' Janggut initiates his moves

We now move on to the story of the Raja of Jeram, Ungku Besar Tun Ahmad Ibn Almarhum Ungku Cik Pandak, who was of the lineage of Long Ghaffar, the founder of Jeram fort.

Before the opening up of Pasir Putih, Jeram was quiet and peaceful. His subjects were respectful towards him. However, after the new district was created, his subjects no longer paid their respects to him. Moreover, the rules and regulations of the new district administration began to curb his activities.

It occurred to him that before long his status as Raja Jeram would come to an end and so he began to think of ways to obstruct the new administration.

He invited to his palace several people whom he thought could assist him in his scheme. Among them were To' Janggut, Haji Said Kampung Marbul, Incik Ishak and Penghulu Adam. After he had shared his thoughts with the four men, they agreed to work to wreck the new administration.

They would instigate the population to dislike the administration on the grounds it was oppressive, as it had imposed various taxes on the ordinary people — such as a dollar's head tax on every person, 12½ sen a year on each fruit tree, three sen on each coconut tree, five sen for each bunch of *sirih* as well as 20 sen on each bullock, 50 sen on each dog and pig, and other taxes on timber such as *temesu*, *medang*, *kuing* and land-tax of 60 sen per acre.

"By pointing out these things to the people, we will achieve our aims," they agreed. With one voice, they pledged to carry out their seditious acts and then each returned to his home.

To' Janggut began his work by going from kampung to kampung. He urged the people to oppose the new laws and rise up to protest the new administration. He succeeded in obtaining the support of 50 per cent of the 2,000 people in Pasir Putih.

The district officers

Well, let us now look at the administration of the district. The first District Officer, Encik Yen, after completing a year's service, returned to Singapore. He was succeeded in 1912 by Nik Salleh from Kota Bharu.[4] Despite the introduction of the new taxes, the district was quiet and peaceful because Nik Salleh had not started collecting the new taxes.

It is possible that the rural people put up with him because he was a Kelantanese. In those days provincialism was still strong in Kelantan. Unfortunately, for the local people, he also served only for a year and then was replaced by Encik Latif, a person from Singapore.

Encik Latif, however, was different from Nik Salleh. He lost no time in enforcing the laws and in collecting the new taxes. Whoever failed to pay the taxes felt the full brunt of his authority. They had to pay fines. If these were not paid immediately the fines would be increased several times the original taxes.

This oppressive authority led to an outbreak of disturbances in several villages. Robberies and violence were rampant. It was a golden opportunity for To' Janggut and his followers who now began to spread their seditious activities.

But the greatest provocation for Ungku Besar and To' Janggut was that they, too, had been ordered to pay the new taxes.

It was especially galling for Ungku Besar because prior to this he had been exempted from paying any tax. This new administration now aroused his ire to a greater degree.

To' Janggut and his followers, therefore, decided to refuse to pay the taxes for the year. This caused the revenue of the district to drop by half. When Encik Latif found out that To' Janggut was responsible, he dispatched Police Sergeant Sulaiman and two other policemen and a detective to take him into custody.

One Friday, as To' Janggut and some 2,000 of his followers were gathered at a *surau* in Kampung Merbul (two miles from Pasir Putih), they took a collective decision to refuse to pay taxes.

The supporters who came from various parts of the district, as far as Bukit Yong, were full of anger against the new administration. News of the gathering became known to Penghulu Awang Jeram who had gone to Pasir Putih to inform Encik Latif.

When the policemen arrived at the scene, they were surprised to find the gathering in a war-like mood. People were armed with various weapons. To' Janggut sat on a platform and later stood up to address the crowd.

As Sergeant Sulaiman pushed his way forward, he asked, "Where is To' Janggut?" The crowd suddenly lapsed into silence, each head turning towards the figure.

"Where is To' Janggut?" he asked again.

To' Janggut identified himself. "I am To' Janggut. Why have you come here? What do you want?"

Sergeant Sulaiman said he had been ordered by the District Officer to ask To' Janggut to appear in Pasir Putih immediately.

But To' Janggut said he could only be there the next day. Sergeant Sulaiman said this could not be allowed.

To' Janggut smiled and moved towards the sergeant. As the crowd watched the seven policemen, To' Janggut said, "Please walk ahead, I'll follow."

Sergeant Sulaiman, however, answered, "No, To' Haji, you walk in front and the policemen will walk behind you."

"There's no way we'll walk in front of you," said To' Janggut. "If we do, it means we're guilty and are your prisoners. We have only been summoned by your chief, so you all walk ahead of us."

In the heat of the argument, and like the legendary Melaka warrior Hang Tuah, To' Janggut pulled out his Minangkabu-style kris from his waist and stabbed Sergeant Sulaiman in the chest. That single thrust caused the sergeant to fall dead.

The crowd encircled the remaining six policemen, disarmed them, and warned them not to resist, otherwise they would be killed, too. They were then told to return to Pasir Putih.

When Encik Latif was informed about the incident by the policemen, he was furious and immediately ordered the nearby villages to be called out to form a force to resist the rebels.

Before any action could be taken, however, someone brought the news that the District Officer and his men should flee to safety. It was rumoured that To' Janggut and his 2,000 followers were on their way, joined by forces loyal to Ungku Besar, who were all armed with guns, knives , spears and machetes. They intended to capture Pasir Putih town.

When he heard this, Encik Latif decided to leave the town with his family and took with him the accounts books. They left in a boat for Semerak, and were determined to reach Kota Bharu. The village chief of Jeram went with him.

After several hours, they arrived at Semerak and the village chief there looked for two or three men to accompany Encik Latif to Kota Bharu. Then the party took off.

The sea journey was rough. The winds were strong and the waves tossed their boat about, making them sick and they began to throw up. The boat nearly capsised as they neared Bachok, but the residents there came to their rescue. Later, in the afternoon, they continued their journey to Kota Bharu, where they unloaded their things.

Encik Latif made straight for the Balai Besar. He sought an audience with the Sultan to whom he reported the details of the previous day's disturbances. He expressed the fear that the rebels under To' Janggut and Ungku Besar might have already taken over the town.

After hearing Encik Latif's report, the Sultan exclaimed, "It looks like To' Janggut and Engku Besar have committed treason." Turning to Encik Latif, he said,

"Tomorrow we will have a meeting with the state officials and you should be present to submit a report on the incident."

Encik Latif withdrew and returned to his house which was crowded with visitors who were anxious to hear from him about the incident. After he had had his bath and taken his meal, he sat down and narrated to them the course of events at Pasir Putih.

One of the listeners said, "This means that the Sultan will suppress To' Janggut and his supporters." Another said, "To' Janggut is not any ordinary person. The conflict will bring suffering to the people of Kelantan like the civil war between Raja Kampung Laut and Raja Kota Bharu long ago, when the ordinary people and all their properties were destroyed."

To return to To' Janggut, he had had ordered his followers to remove the body of Sergeant Sulaiman and bury it at Merbul. He told them to get ready to attack Pasir Putih town that very night in order to punish the District Officer. He told the crowd, "Our men outnumber their forces. Remember we will fight and put up resistance in order to put down tyranny and oppression."

About eight o'clock that night the combined forces of To' Janggut and Ungku Besar began moving towards Pasir Putih town in three directions. The first group headed towards north of the town under Haji Said, another led by Panglima Encik Ishak Merbul headed northeast, and the last under To' Janggut went towards southwest of Pasir Putih, followed in the rear by Ungku Besar Jeram and his followers, who carried food and weapons.

At half past nine they arrived at Pasir Putih town. On the orders of To' Janggut, his supporters broke down the jail-house and the house of Encik Latif, with loud shouts and firing of gunshots. Thus, Pasir Putih town fell into the hands of To' Janggut and Ungku Besar and their forces.

To' Janggut's uprising against the Government

Ungku Besar was declared the ruler of Pasir Putih, while To' Janggut was made his chief minister, Haji Said his second-in-command, Penghulu Jeram Syahbandar and Encik Ishak the District Officer.

To' Janggut, however, urged caution. In order that they should not lose the people's support, he urged his followers not to act recklessly. "Let us not commit any destruction in Limbungan. We are not angry with the Sultan. We are only angry with the oppressive District Officer. If we commit further destruction, we will certainly come into conflict with the authorities in Kota Bharu."

"I am sure Encik Latif has already reported to His Royal Highness, who is bound to send his police and troops to Pasir Putih."

Ungku Besar returned to his palace in Jeram, which he preferred to Pasir Putih, leaving To' Janggut to manage matters in the town.

A few days passed when an emissary of the Sultan suddenly appeared at Ungku Besar's palace, seeking an audience. His name was To' Seri. He informed Ungku Besar that he had been sent by the Mentri Besar (Chief Minister), Datok Seri Setia Raja, Datuk Hulubalang Kadok, Datuk Panglima Perang Lundang and other chiefs who awaited the Jeram chief at Padang Pak Amat (a village two miles from Jeram) at the house of Iman Kadir.

"What is the purpose of this meeting?" asked Ungku Besar.

To which To' Seri replied, "There is something important to discuss with Your Highness as the presence of these members indicate their importance."

Ungku Besar asked when the meeting was to take place, and was told immediately if he could oblige them. He turned to To' Janggut and asked whether he should go to the meeting.

"Yes, we should go," said To' Janggut. "We should find out what they want. We should not be afraid because we have done no wrong and have not opposed the Sultan but only the oppression of Encik Latif, the District Officer."

Whereupon Ungku Besar arose and the whole gathering started to move towards Padang Pak Amat.

However, on their arrival there, they found that the Ministers and chiefs had returned to Kota Bharu but had left behind a representative, Che Su, who was ordered to hear their grievances and report back to them.

It is possible that the Mentri Besar and his delegation had withdrawn from the scene because they feared that To' Janggut's forces outnumbered them, or probably thought they should avert a military confrontation. The latter was more likely and reflected the shrewdness of the Mentri Besar.

"Your Highness," addressed Che Su, "what are the reasons which have led to this unrest in Pasir Putih?"

To which Ungku Besar replied, "I think it's best that you ask the people gathered here. You should hear it from their own mouths rather than from me."

A villager named Haji Senik from Kampung Gong Datuk said that the following reasons had led the people to rebel against the District Officer:

First, his administration is oppressive and cruel, unlike the previous District Officers. He often abused and swore at people with harsh words...

Second, we do not like our state to be governed by a foreigner (from Singapore) as a District Officer because it goes against our local customs.

Third, we prefer an administration under royalty because royalty have ruled our country from early times.

Fourthly, the regulations on taxes are punitive especially the taxes on cattle, produce and land, which cause us hardships. Moreover, any delay in payment of taxes means fines added to our burdern.

Fifthly, during the reigns of royalty, the taxes were not so harsh. Now no one is exempted from paying taxes, and if there is non-payment the properties are seized.

"We hope the authorities will consider our grievances, especially with regard to taxes which most of us cannot afford to pay. Please convey our demands to the authorities in Kota Bharu and urge them to consider them sympathetically. We do not intend to make trouble unnecessarily."

After this address, the meeting broke up. Everyone returned to their houses.

The following day, Encik Su, Iman Kadir and Penghulu Pak Amat left for Kota Bharu and on their arrival there went to the istana, where they were granted an audience by the Sultan. The ministers were also present.

After he had heard their report, the Sultan was angry with Ungku Besar and To' Janggut and their followers. He ordered a bale of red cloth be given to Encik Su and ordered him to cut out from it arm-bands to levees who would pledge loyalty to him. Those who refused to wear them were to be branded as "traitors" and be taken into custody.

A notice was also to be issued to this effect: "Be it known that Ungku Besar Tan Ahmad Jeram, To' Janggut, Al-Haji Said Merbul, Encik Ishak and Penghulu Adam, the heads of organised bands, must surrender themselves within seven days, failing which they would be arrested and sentenced to death."

Two days after this announcement, and the handing out of arm-bands to the Sultan's loyal levees, it was found that many among To' Janggut's supporters had refused to follow the orders.

News of the outbreak spread further when another notice appeared announcing as follows: "Anyone who arrests Ungku Besar, To' Janggut, Haji Said, Haji Ishak and Penghulu Adam will receive a reward of $500.00."

On hearing this, Ungku Besar, To' Janggut and the other rebel leaders consulted their followers whether they should give themselves up or continue their struggle. It was decided to continue with their resistance.

As the rebels prepared to resist the forces of the Sultan from Kota Bharu, the Sultan and his Ministers heard of the increased strength of the rebel following and were worried that they could not deal with them.

Consequently, they decided to ask the British authorities in Singapore for military assistance.

British troops intervene to quell To' Janggut's rebellion
A letter for assistance was sent by the British Adviser, J. Davis Mason,[5] to the Governor, Sir Arthur Henderson Young since Kelantan was a British protectorate.

At this moment Britain was in the midst of the First World War in Europe. The Governor ordered the Commander of British armed forces in Singapore to send about 1,500 troops[6] in a British warship to Kelantan.

On 10 May 1915 the troops from Singapore landed at Kota Bharu, and their commander later met with Sultan Mohamed IV.

After two days in the capital, the troops began their march to Pasir Putih via Gunung. News of their departure reached Ungku Besar and To' Janggut.

The rebels decided to avoid any military confrontation with them. They advised their followers to disappear from the scene.

On the night of 13 May the British soldiers reached Pasir Putih. Next day they began a search of every village to look for the ring-leaders, but could not find them. They had disappeared into the jungle, but were kept informed on the activities of the troops.

For four nights the troops encamped at Pasir Putih. On the 17 May they decided to pull out and started their trek back to Kota Bharu, where they remained for about a week awaiting news of rebel activities and then embarked on the warship to return to Singapore, where German enemy boats were said to be active owing to the European war.

The arrival of Indian troops in Kelantan
Several days after the withdrawal of British troops, To' Janggut and his followers re-emerged from their hiding and seized back Pasir Putih town.

This news reached the ears of the authorities in Kota Bharu. After they had conferred among themselves, the Sultan and the British Adviser sent a request to Singapore to ask for further military assistance. This came in the form of Indian troops and a small force of Singapore Malay Volunteers.

The troops under British officers arrived in June and after a night's march appeared in Pasir Putih. Next day they began hunting for To' Janggut and others on the wanted list, but were unable to find them.

In their anger, they burnt Jeram town. The houses of To' Janggut, Encik Ishak and Al-Haji Said were put to the flames as well as nine houses belonging to Ungku Besar. They seized numerous personal items and goods from the houses such as padi and also the elephants of Ungku Besar, and then returned to Pasir Putih to await the arrival of To' Janggut.

True enough, on the night of 25 June, their fury aroused by the burnings, To' Janggut and 1,000 of his supporters emerged, armed with guns and traditional weapons and marched from Jeram to Pasir Putih.

As they entered the town, they fired gunshots and let out shouts, which sounded like thunderbolts. After some firing, To' Janggut ordered his followers to retreat to the village of Kampung Saring.

On 26 June, the Indian troops came out of the town towards their direction and as they neared the village, both sides exchanged fire.

Readers would understand that in this confrontation To' Janggut and his supporters were no match for the better-trained and well-equipped Indian soldiers, even though they outnumbered the latter.

Thus, in the fighting which ensued, many of the villagers and supporters of To' Janggut were killed. Seeing this, many of his supporters fled.

But To' Janggut, Abas Berani, Husin Harimau, Awang Ngah and Abdul Rahman Anak Kerbau and several others stood their ground and kept firing at their enemy. This so enraged the Indian troops who, with fixed bayonets, charged at them, killing most of them.

Thus, fell To' Janggut due to the superior fighting prowess of his enemy.

The body of To' Janggut was taken to Kota Bahru.

The troops gave out an order that all the corpses should be buried except that of To' Janggut which was to be taken to Kota Bahru to be shown before the Sultan. All Kelantan was shaken by the news that To' Janggut had been killed in the fighting with Indian troops.

As the body was carried by a bullock-cart all the way from Pasir Putih to Kota Bahru, the road was lined with people including women and children who came out to watch the sight.

At Kota Bahru more people came out to the streets to see what would happen as the corpse was taken to the Istana. The Sultan ordered that it be shown around the town for the people to learn the fate of anyone who dared to defy the Sultan and his government.

At every street and alley in Kota Bahru people who viewed the body wept, while some said it was right the government should punish those who rebelled against its authority, but all sorts of talk were stirred up.

Finally, the bullock-cart arrived at the Padang Bank, a field in front of the Sultan's palace. The corpse was lifted up, head down, legs tied up, three times.

This in the Kelantanese dialect was called *sait* and the people were ordered to watch by assembling at the scene. It should be remembered that in the past this was the punishment meted out by the rajas to those who committed *derhaka*.

When the body had been *sait*, it was taken down and ordered to be transported across the river to Pasir Pekan and there it was buried. The grave has become a shrine and is revered by many people. Thus, ends the story of To' Janggut's war and his martyrdom.

* * *

The Ballad of To' Janggut

To' Janggut a native of Kelantan
Was born in Kampung Jeram
His fighting courage was no mere fiction
It fired the people's imagination
He exhorted the people to rise up against the state
Moving about tirelessly hither and thither
With shrewdness and intelligence
He attracted thousands of followers
News of his rebellion finally reached the capital
The military commanders were sent out
As the forces of both sides met
They fearlessly charged and fired at one another
To' Janggut's men engaged a superior enemy
The battle at Kubu Batas Besar
Was between the soldiers of a modern army
And To' Janggut's traditional brave warriors
Many of whom were injured
As one fighter fell, another took his place
To prevent his forces from wavering,
To' Janggut cried out, "Advance!"
Enemy troops fired incessantly
Many more fighters fell, causing alarm and dismay,
An enraged To' Janggut yelled, "Ya Allah"
Slashed at the enemy on his left and right
But a bullet hit him
Felling his body to the ground
As he lay dead, his followers fled and dispersed
Indian troops rushed towards the corpse
Bound the hands and feet and lifted it away.
The body was taken to the capital
And placed before the military chief
In Kota Bharu it was exhibited
Then carried around the town
And finally ended up at the town square

Hung legs up and head down
Crowds watched this spectacle
As if the corpse was being roasted
For an hour it was exposed
Many people in the crowd
Choked in their throats and could not hold back their tears
The corpse was brought down
And carried to Pasir Pekan for burial.
This verse is penned in the memory of
To' Janggut the brave warrior
Who received retribution for fighting for independence.

Part II

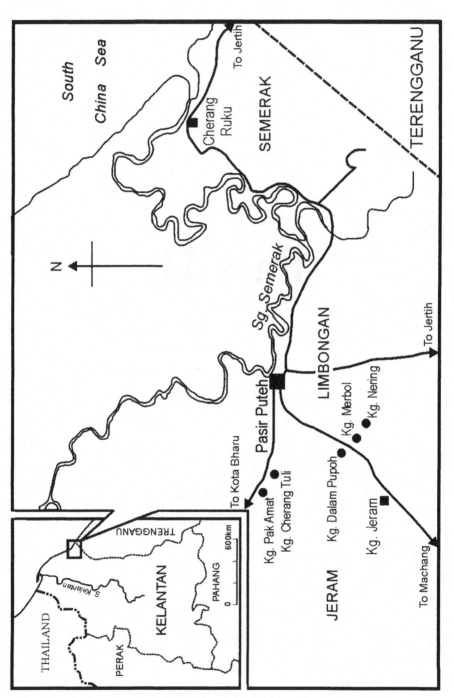

Map of the Pasir Puteh Area

Chapter 5

Newspaper Versions of the Rebellion of 1915: Was There a "Rising" in Kelantan?

> The death of To' Janggut, leader of the Kelantan rebels, was no doubt an unpleasant surprise for the old ruffian's friends, and may do some good in shaking the ridiculous belief still held by many Malays in the efficacy of life-preserving charms.
>
> — *The Straits Times*, 31 May 1915

Introduction

The following is an account of the 1915 rebellion as seen by the newspapers in British Malaya. Newspaper reports of the event were fragmentary, vague and sometimes contradictory. As news censorship was imposed because of the war in Europe, the newspapers relied on government or military communiqués issued in Singapore for information about local and international events. Their own coverage of domestic activities was woefully inadequate, as most did not have regional correspondents and were forced to depend on the occasional reports sent in by their readers.

The "rising" at Pasir Putih clearly raised problems of terminology for the newspapers that reported the incident. The list of terms used started with "trouble", followed by "outbreak", "disturbance", "riot", "unrest" and finally the controversial "rising". Those taking part in the "rising" were variously described as "rioters", "disaffected Malays", "insurgents" and "rebels". In the end, doubts were raised over whether there had been, in fact, any "rising" at all. To' Janggut's name appeared in reports announcing his death, with comments on his reputation for invulnerability, providing oblique recognition of what would later become a defining feature of his legend.

But To' Janggut's "personal war" went unnoticed. Neither was there any indication of the severity of the "scorched earth" policies carried out by the British troops on the rebels' houses and properties or the harshness of the British authorities' treatment of his corpse. The British major newspapers in the United Kingdom paid scant attention to the rebellion, as they were more concerned with events in Europe. In sharp contrast, only a small section of the British public was informed about the rebellion when a photograph of the public display of his corpse reached the London office of a radical newspaper, *Truth,* which published it with "some caustic comments on the brutal things that were done in the name of the British Empire in the dark corners of the earth".[1]

Reports of the Outbreak

The newspapers of British Malaya had previously portrayed Kelantan as a quiet, rural backwater. When the state suddenly experienced an explosion of violence, death and destruction, newspaper reports from the region were initially unclear and most of the population of Malaya did not receive full information about the event.

Although the "rising" at Pasir Putih took place on 29 April 1915, the newspapers only learned about it on 2 May when the Singapore authorities decided to send a military force by sea to Kelantan. Further information reached the major cities and towns of Malaya very slowly because the network of local newspaper correspondents was still woefully small and inadequate. Gradually, more information emerged. British troops were landing in Kelantan, and European women and children in Kota Bharu, the state capital, were being evacuated to a border village in southern Thailand. The newspapers began pressing the authorities for more information.

On 3 May *The Straits Times* published an official communique issued by Military Command headquarters in Fort Canning, Singapore. It said, "A local disturbance had broken out at Pasir Putih, about 25 miles south by east of Kota Bharu, due, it is reported, to a disinclination on the part of inhabitants to pay their taxes. As a precautionary measure, a military party has been sent from Singapore and a warship will probably proceed to the vicinity of Kota Bharu to give assistance if required."

On 4 May *The Straits Times* carried another brief official statement issued in Singapore with the consent of the Governor, which stated, "Affairs in Kelantan are not likely to take any serious aspect, the disturbance, which was purely local, being practically at an end." In an editorial, of the same date, entitled, "Another warning…," the newspaper referred to the Kelantan incident and urged the setting up of a European civil defence force to protect Europeans in times of an emergency:

The following day, 5 May, the newspaper reported that the Sultan of Trengganu had left for an official visit to Kelantan.

On 7 May *The Straits Times* carried a lengthy report by an "Eye-witness on the spot", who was clearly a European correspondent. This report was reproduced in the Penang-based newspaper, *The Straits Echo*, the following day. The newspaper said the report might be taken as "an official account" of what had happened in Pasir Putih. The correspondent had met the British Adviser to get the facts about how "a *rising* of the Malays" had taken place at Pasir Putih, and then narrated the events that ensued.

The correspondent reported that since 1 January 1915, the people of the district had been required to pay a land tax instead of a produce tax, adding, "the former is very light and less oppressive than the latter". There had been some difficulty, however, in collecting this tax. At a public meeting held in a village where the people objected to the payment, a police sergeant told them that they must go with him to the court to explain to the A.D.O. (Assistant District Officer), Che Latif, described as "a Jawi Pekan". (Latif was, in fact, the D.O. A "Jawi Pekan" was a local-born of mixed Malay-Indian parentage.) The people apparently objected, so he handcuffed an elderly Malay and was about to lead him away when the man's son, one of the ringleaders in the dispute, stabbed the sergeant, killing him. When the A.D.O. was informed, he sent six policemen to arrest the murderer, but on seeing the threatening attitude of the people, they ran away. The A.D.O. then took all the money in the Treasury and fled with his family to Kota Bharu to report the matter to the British Adviser and the Sultan. The rest of the report described how the "*rebels*" had destroyed files at government offices, burnt down two shop-houses, and looted the bungalows of European planters. The group was rumoured to be moving on to the state capital.

On the same day the newspaper published a short item that referred to British Adviser Langham-Carter's Annual Report for 1913, which explained the state's proposed plan to collect land-rents and fees. The newspaper commented that such information "may explain the cause of the recent trouble in the State which it has been officially stated is due to a disinclination on the part of the inhabitants to pay their taxes".

On 8 May the *Utusan Melayu,* a Singapore-based Malay daily, which published in the Jawi script and was the sister daily of the English-language *Singapore Free Press,* carried the same item for its Malay readers. It used the words *kacau* and *huru hara,* which both can be translated as "disturbance", to describe the episode.

On 9 May *The Straits Times* reported the arrival of the Sultan of Trengganu in Kelantan by motor boat from Besut (Trengganu) to begin his official visit. "His Highness enjoyed the trip and looked very well," said the report. "The troubles at Kelantan slightly disturbed the equanimity of the excursion, but not to any serious extent, and all the party were pleased with their reception at Kelantan."

On 12 May a statement issued by Command Headquarters in Singapore said that the British force had reached Pasir Putih near the Semarak River without opposition. The country was reported to be quiet. The *"insurgents"* appeared to have dispersed, but it was thought advisable to leave a small force to maintain order.

On 15 June *The Straits Times* carried a long report quoting extracts from Langham-Carter's 1914 Annual Report on Kelantan. The daily said it was "of more than ordinary interest in view of the late *unrest,* which had its source in tax-collecting difficulties". The Report indicated that the state had incurred a "considerable deficit" and was adopting a "policy of marking time" with regard to the collection of land revenue. Despite the deficit, land revenue collected in 1914 was about $100,000, $33,000 less than estimated more than in the previous year. At the time of framing the estimates, it was hoped that during the whole of the year under review the new land tax system, which introduced a fixed land rent in place of payment of produce taxes, would have been in operation. It said revenues did not meet expectations because the system could not be put into regular operation during the year. Numerous cases of dishonesty on the part of revenue collectors detected by the Land Department were also partly to blame. In Ulu Kelantan and Pasir Putih districts, land rent collections had increased from native holdings, before the general adoption of the principle of fixed rents.

On 16 and 17 June *The Straits Times* presented further extracts from W. Langham-Carter's 1914 Annual Report. The story that appeared on 16 June spoke of a decline of local handicrafts in Kelantan, and mentioned that at the outbreak of the war in Europe in early 1914, practically all Europeans and a good proportion of the non-Malayan members of the clerical staff had enlisted as special constables, and received military training. The 17 June report referred to the Kelantan census in 1911, which said that out of the 270,000 Malays in Kelantan, a very large proportion were padi growers and smallholders.

On 20 May *The Straits Times* reported that it was a "reassuring sign" that the "white troops" sent to Kelantan to deal with the "*disturbance*" exactly a fortnight ago had returned to Singapore. This report, reproduced in *The Straits Echo* on 22nd May, referred initially to those taking part as "disaffected Malays", and twice characterised them as "rebels". A British warship anchored off the mouth of the Semerak River, near Pasir Putih, was reported to have fired 4-inch shells in the direction of Pasir Putih, some seven miles inland, but failed to hit Pasir Putih. The shells apparently did no damage, but according to one official, "created the utmost consternation". Overall, the army's tour of duty was uneventful. They did not make any contact with the "rebels", and it was therefore decided to withdraw the "white troops". Their duties in Pasir Putih had been taken over by the Malay States Guides, which consisted mainly of Sikh soldiers.

On 27 May under the heading, "Kelantan Trouble", *The Straits Times* published a brief communique from Military Headquarters, stating: "On Sunday night, the rebels (in Kelantan) made a feeble attack. The Malay States Guides detachment dispersed them, killing four and wounding at least two. Toh (sic) Janggut, a rebel leader, is among the killed. One Sikh of the M.S.G. was superficially wounded. Attempts are being made to locate further bodies of rebels."

On the same day the Malay daily, *Utusan Melayu,* carried a similar item under the headlines, "*Kelantan huru hara di Pasir Putih. To' Janggut terbunuh* (Kelantan. Disturbance in Pasir Putih. To' Janggut killed).

On 29 May, all major English-language newspapers carried a lengthy official account of the skirmish that said the "rebel" leader, To' Janggut, had been killed by the Malay States Guides. *The Straits Times* report used the word "rebel" to describe the leader in its headline as follows: "Kelantan Trouble. The Outbreak and How it was Suppressed. Rebel leader killed". But the detailed report used the terms "rioter" or "rioters" throughout to describe those taking part in the incident, which it termed an "outbreak" or "riot". The anonymous writer of the report was actually W. George Maxwell, the Acting Secretary to the High Commissioner, who had been sent out to investigate the incident. He specifically made it a point to stress that a "general rising" had been averted largely due to the government's action.

Maxwell's report said that although the "riot" was confined to the Pasir Putih district, messages were reportedly sent by two leaders, Ungku Besar and To' Janggut, to various people in other parts of the state urging them to make a simultaneous rising. At Pasir Mas, a gang of men set fire to a railway clerk's quarters on 6 May, and shot at the European troops when they were putting out the fire. In Ulu Kelantan district, a gang of 17 armed men was seen in a village, and elsewhere a number of cattle thieves and gang-robbers not only from Kelantan but also from Trengganu did what they could to terrify the villagers throughout the state, hoping to profit from the general panic.

Following the departure of the European troops, the official report went on, everything was quiet in Pasir Putih. Shopkeepers and villagers who had fled to the neighbouring district of Besut, in the state of Trengganu, began to return. W.E. Pepys assumed charge as District Officer of Pasir Putih. Chief Inspector Jackson remained to lead the police investigation. The five leaders, Ungku Besar, To' Janggut, Penghulu Adam, Che Ishak and Haji Shaid, were called upon by public proclamation to surrender within seven days. Only one of them, Penghulu Adam, did so.

When the seven days were up, the houses of the other four leaders were burnt, and a reward of $500 for the arrest of any one of them was offered by the Government. It was believed that all four men were in Trengganu territory. Permission to enter Trengganu in search of them was being sought from the Trengganu Government.

On 31 May the editorial page of *The Straits Times* carried a small commentary on the death of To' Janggut and the end of his alleged invulnerability. The writer said: "The death of To' Janggut, leader of the Kelantan rebels, was no doubt an unpleasant surprise for the old ruffian's friends, and may do some good in shaking the ridiculous belief still held by many Malays in the efficacy of life-preserving charms. It should prove that a .308 bullet is much more up to its work than any amount of amulets and atmospheres. Still, hard-held superstitions are slow to kill."

On 25 June *The Straits Times* and *The Straits Echo* both carried a letter from a correspondent ("an old resident") questioning the official report published on 19 May. The letter was published in the form of a news report under the headline, "Kelantan. Some observations on recent troubles. Story of "Rising" denied." The editor of *The Straits Times* prefaced the report with some remarks of his own to indicate the newspaper's stand, as follows:

> It seems to be generally recognised now that there was a good deal of unwarranted apprehension over the discontent that arose in some parts of Kelantan with reference to the collection of taxes. The startling tales of thousands of armed Malays "gives furiously to smiles" those who know the country intimately and are familiar with the essentially peaceful character of the people. We have received some notes from an old resident on the report, officially prepared, which was recently issued to the press, and these seem to deserve careful consideration.

Based on "an intimate knowledge of the Malays of the district", the correspondent declared,

> I have no hesitation in affirming that no evidence has been produced to show that there was any *rising*. He dismissed the official account of the murder of the police sergeant. We cannot accept the story — it is against all reason for anyone with a knowledge of Malays to believe that they had gone a few yards, and then stabbed the sergeant. Much more probable that some indignity was offered to To' Janggut that caused him to lose his temper and approach

in a state of *"amok"* — no Malay sergeant single handed could have induced 20 Malays to go with him if they had been gathered together for purposes of resistance.

The correspondent said that when he questioned the planters, they admitted they only had "rumours" to go on, and even eight hours after they had fled, their bungalows remained intact. "It transpires the rioters did not burn any Government buildings at Pasir Putih or Semerak, and as far as reliable evidence goes the damage done at Semerak was caused by Malays living close to the bungalows, and in their houses large quantities of booty were found," he said. The looting was interrupted by the arrival of a warship. He also said Police Inspector Jackson, "acting on Malay information, sent back sensational reports" about alleged numbers of "rebels", although he had not seen them personally. They were alleged to be entrenched, but no trench, stockade fence or other obstacle was ever encountered.

"To Inspector Jackson's action, coupled with the flight of the Europeans from Semerak..., we can ascribe the pillaging. Beyond that nothing did occur that could be called a *riot*, let alone a *rising*," he repeated, and then added,

> On one of the most peaceful of our protectorates a quite unjustifiable slur has been cast and no effort seems to be made to show quite clearly that Kelantan always was and is absolutely a safe and peaceful country, inhabited by probably the gentlest Malays of the whole peninsula. Following on the Singapore mutiny one might think Europeans were not safe, but life and property are absolutely safe and always were. In my years of residence in the district, as the first settler, I never thought of carrying revolvers or of having watchmen. It is impossible for anyone with a knowledge of these natives to conceive such a thing as a "rising".
>
> I repeat, anyone interested in Kelantan either having relations or friends or investments can accept the assurance of those who have lived there for years that there never was a "rising" and never can be, provided a firm government is at the head of affairs and the lost prestige of the white man is regained.... It is a pity that any alleged opposition attacks or assemblies should have taken place in parts where the Political Officer (Farrer) who went with the troops was not present, as he is a man who thoroughly understands Malays and appears to have found no signs of a "rising".

Owing to all that has happened, the finances of the country, which were in a bad state before, will be further burdened with heavy cost of a totally unnecessary naval and military expedition and investors will be chary of a country in which a "rising" has taken place. That is why I am so anxious that the actual facts should be made known as widely as possible. In the interests of the country, it is most necessary to remove as far and as quickly as possible the false impressions and the groundless anxieties that have been created.

Thereafter, the major newspapers seemed to lose interest in the affair. It was left to the Malay daily, *Utusan Melayu,* to continue reporting on incidents relating to the mopping-up operations by the Malay States Guides in the rural areas of Kelantan and the punitive actions taken by the British authorities against those "rebels" who were caught.

Whether or not the public had become confused on the true nature of the incident, British officials were increasingly clear about what it was. The Governor, the British Adviser W. Langham-Carter and his successor all considered the incident a "rising".

In the Annual Report for Kelantan for 1915, R.J. Farrer, who had taken over as Acting British Adviser for Kelantan, wrote:

The Pasir Puteh [sic] Rising has been so frequently and fully discussed that any further description thereof seems out of place. It is sufficient to say that it broke out on 29th April in consequence of the murder by To' Janggut of a Sergeant of Police, and that a band of rebels headed by Ungku Besar and the murderer then descended upon and sacked Pasir Puteh (the District Officer having left by boat with the Treasury contents). Thereafter anarchy reigned in that district until the arrival of the Force from Singapore, and the disitrict was almost deserted until To' Janggut's death in a so-called attack on the Malay States Guides restored confidence.[2]

Chapter 6

The People of Pasir Putih Relate the Causes of To' Janggut's Dissatisfaction and Identify the Ringleaders

I hear that To' Janggut got a letter from the *orang hilir* (which he explains as) Tungku Chik Penambang, saying that people were to keep back their taxes... I asked Tok Kueng Puteh when the letter had come and he said, "Quite recently." He said To' Janggut had gone himself to Kota Bahru and brought it back to Pasir Putih. If it was known that I had told this secret, I should be killed.

— Dolah Timun to Pepys, 7 July 1915

Introduction

According to the results of an enquiry conducted in Pasir Putih by British officials in 1915 on the causes of the rebellion, local inhabitants did not construe the events as the result of To' Janggut's personal war. Contrary to later versions of the local folk legend, informants did not view Ungku Besar as To' Janggut's patron, but instead named a palace aristocrat, Tungku Chik Penambang, as "the head of the rebellion wishing to depose the Sultan and succeed him after getting rid of all Europeans and other *orang luar* (foreigners)". Tungku Chik Penambang was said to have ordered To' Janggut to carry out the attack in Pasir Putih "with the approval of all the Tungkus in Kota Bahru except the Sultan and his sons". According to these informants, Tungku Chik Penambang and the "Tungkus" in Kota Bahru appeared to have been exploiting local dissatisfaction over the new land taxes and the allegedly harsh methods of tax collection carried out by the former District Officer, Abdul Latif.

76

The Official Enquiry

The colonial administration did not often have occasion to conduct an enquiry into the causes of an uprising, but the British Adviser, W. Langham-Carter, decided to take the initiative to find out the causes of the people's dissatisfaction, and to determine who the real ringleaders were. Three other British officials — the Singapore Governor's political officer, R.J. Farrer, the Chief Police Inspector, G. Jackson, and the District Officer of Pasir Putih, W.E. Pepys — joined Langham-Carter in interviewing some 30 people to find out their views on the event. In the survey report, To' Janggut appears as a prominent fighter, but not the overall leader. The survey was initiated while the British troops were in the midst of confronting To' Janggut and the rebels, and was concluded a month after his death. The results were not made public.[1]

Langham-Carter was determined to get to the bottom of the causes of the rebellion because his own career was on the line. The rebellion was tied to local opposition to the new land tax, which he had just introduced. According to Langham-Carter's own account of the rebellion, there had been few indications of the people's dissatisfaction over the new land tax, but they had clearly disliked the earlier produce taxes that were now abolished and replaced with a land rent. According to Langham-Carter, the rebellion had taken him by surprise. Apparently, he had been expecting the people to welcome rather than oppose the new land tax.

In a report forwarded by the Governor in Singapore to the Colonial Office in London, Langham-Carter quoted the words of the people he and the other British officials had interviewed.[2] In some instances, officials set down remarks or observations on the views of the interviewee. For the purpose of clarification, I have added additional comments, wherever necessary, in the footnotes, or in square brackets.

The most revealing information that emerges from these interviews is the general misapprehension of the people about the new land tax. It became clear to these British officials that the people had believed that the new tax was meant to be levied in addition to the previous "unpopular" produce taxes. Most of the people were unaware that the earlier produce taxes had been abolished under the new system. The unpopularity of the District Officer, Encik Abdul Latif is also highlighted in most of the interviews, giving the impression that he was insensitive and high-handed as a magistrate and tax collector.

There had apparently been a miscommunication of the intentions of the new tax on the part of the District Office, for which Langham-Carter and the D.O. were later held responsible. To their dismay, the British officials discovered that some who would have to pay more taxes had decided to tell the peasants that they would have to pay the new tax on top of existing taxes. The confusion they spread aroused the provincial loyalties and disaffection of the Kelantanese against "foreigners" — the D.O. from Singapore, the British officials and the Sikh policemen.

Ungku Besar, the feudal chief of Pasir Putih, and other aristocrats in the state capital of Kota Bharu were identified as the "unseen" ringleaders behind the outbreak. Among them were members of the Kelantan royalty — Tungku Chik Penambang, Tungku Petra Dalam Kebun, and Tungku Sri Mas. An informant, Tuan Muda, told Pepys: "Ungku Besar who informed my man, Teh Wan Nik of the intended attack on Pasir Putih at 5 a.m. tomorrow morning [24 May 1915] also told him that Tungku Chik Penambang was ordering the attack and that it was with the approval of all the Tungkus in Kota Bahru except the Sultan and his sons."[3]

Another informant, Nebing Tok Dolah of Jeram, a village chief, also disclosed to Pepys how Ungku Besar tried to solicit support of other Tungkus: "Two days after the attack on Pasir Putih (on 29 April 1915) Ungku Besar came to my house. I asked him what is the cause of this disturbance? He replied that he consulted the Tungku Perkoma Rajah as to the people's difficulties about taxes and the latter said that if the people had no money to pay at present they could hang on (and pay later when they had). I replied, "That is excellent advice but does not explain the violence." Ungku Besar replied, "To' Janggut insists on fighting all the same."

It appears that British officials prodded some of those they interviewed to name the "ringleaders". Some volunteered information willingly, while others were cautious and refused to say much, but the information collected indicated that To' Janggut did not act alone and that he was not considered the mastermind behind the rising.

The interviewees did provide information about the views of To' Janggut on several issues. They reported that he frequently was heard railing against the produce taxes, against the District Officer, against the white men and against the British troops.

The memorandum that Langham-Carter submitted to the Governor along with his report defended his policies. He denied the alleged harshness of the District Officer in collecting taxes or the introduction of the new land-rent as causes of the rising. He claimed that he had sent out 1,000 pamphlets in the Malay Jawi script, and none of the peasants had said, "We do not understand the new land rules." After reading over the statements of the interviewees, he concluded that the causes of the rebellion were the "inability, neglect or refusal" of the people to pay the old produce taxes, and that "they had been led to believe that the opportunity for refusal had come".[4] He believed that the people of Pasir Putih were encouraged by people from outside the district to rise up against the old taxes.

> I have taken a number of statements myself and I put from these and from those taken by others extracts of all which a hasty perusal of a mass of documents shows bear on causes. I found, as did also Mr Pepys, an extraordinary difficulty in getting any cause alleged for the rising. It was, indeed, only after passing before the deponents the various alleged cases that a selection of one or more was made. Had the cause really been the innovation of a land-tax to be collected at some time or other from almost all people, it must have been within the knowledge of all that this was the grievance common to all and it must have been put forward practically unanimously and in the very front line of all. The extracts tell to me, however, so plain a tale that I will not analyse them in detail, but I wish to lay special stress on the two marked "A" and "M" which set out that people came from outside Pasir Puteh to inform the people of Pasir Puteh that the land tax was hard.
>
> It is abundantly clear from the extracts that much of the old-taxes due for 1914 had not been paid; and that there had been inability, neglect or refusal to pay these is confirmed by the fact that the District Officer had found it necessary to issue ... three times as many notices [demanding payment] as were issued in 1913.... Merely from the extracts I think it is plain that the District Officer was not collecting taxes old or new, current or in arrears, with any harshness. It has, I think, very great significance that one of the

5 Pasir Puteh leaders (Penghulu Adam, see extract IV) was himself under summons to pay produce taxes due in 1914 and that To' Janggut another of the five leaders resented this. It is definitely given as the reason for the attack on Pasir Puteh.

...but there was in addition among some of the rebels at least a very active desire to turn out the non-Kelantanese, that this could not be resisted by the non-Kelantanese forces, and that no others were believed to be available is shown quite clearly by extracts K2, B, G, etc. It is fairly plain that no resistance was looked for from the Malay Police and events justified expectations in various places, but whether or how far the Malay Police were tampered with by the promoters I cannot say.[5]

The Interviews

The following section contains extracts from statements given by interviewees. The statements were included in a report compiled by the British Adviser, W. Langham-Carter.[6] They are under two separate headings.

(a) People's commentary on To' Janggut and taxes

"C" Statement of Police Constable Awang [probably recorded by Jackson; no date]:

> "To' Janggut complained about heavy taxes this year. He also said the District Officer was very hard on the people. If the soldiers dare not come, they would pay no taxes and the country would be governed by Ungku Besar."

"G" Statement of Daraman bin Daid, recorded by Pepys on 25th May 1915:

> "To' Janggut said, 'Let us kill the white men and the Sikhs. It is hard for the people while they are here."

"I" Statement of Tuan Muda, recorded by W.L.C. on 12th May 1915:

> "I had heard To' Janggut say the District Officer was hard over the padi and other taxes trying to collect them all at one time instead of separately...."

"N" Statement of Che Sahid (to Jackson on 19 May 1915):

> "I was advised to run away as To' Janggut said he would murder all foreigners."

"P" Statement of H. Daud, school master of Pasir Putih, recorded by Jackson on 11 May 1915:

> "My boys told me if To' Janggut's people met any non-Kelantanese they were going to murder them because the non-Kelantanese including Europeans want to rule the country — and I, being Selangor born, was afraid..."

"W" Statement of Nebing Awang of Nering, a village chief, to Pepys on 3 June 1915:

> "When I went round alone on the night of 28th April I saw To' Janggut and Penghulu Adam on the road at Nering. I was afraid to stop and talk to them as both were angry with me because earlier in this year I had served a summons on Penghulu Adam [one of the rebel leaders] to pay padi-tax for 1914. To' Janggut, a life-long friend of his, resented this. I overheard them saying, "We are going to get all the people together to make an attack on Pasir Puteh town." I heard them go on, "because of the summons which was served on Penghulu Adam." Three days before I had passed To' Janggut's house and heard his voice and that of Penghulu Adam and Che Sahak. I heard them saying, "We will attack when convenient." Penghulu Adam was a constant visitor at To' Janggut's house, so too was Che Sahak. H. Said was a new friend. He had been going there in the month preceding. The above were always plotting. That is what aroused suspicions. Penghulu Adam is a head cattle thief, not doing the stealing himself. He had several agents...

(b) People's commentary on the involvement of certain Tunkus in the rising

"P" Statement of H. Daud (to Pepys on 24th May 1915):

> "At 8.30 p.m. I heard from Semerak men whom I don't know that all the Sikhs and white men have been killed and that Tunku Chik of Penambang is now at Kuala Semerak having arrived last evening."

"V" Statement of Abdul Latif, the District Officer of Pasir Putih to Pepys on 23 May 1915:

> "I have heard both in Kota Bahru and Pasir Puteh that Tungku Chik Penambang is the head of the rebellion wishing to depose H.H. the Sultan and succeed him after getting rid of all Europeans and other *orang luar* (foreigners)."

"Y" Statement of Che Mat, Chief Clerk at District Office of Pasir Putih to Pepys on 26 June 1915:

> "When I was going to Kota Bahru from Pasir Puteh after the first attack, I met near Gunong some men who asked me whether it was true Pasir Puteh was sacked. They said, "This is not the people's doing. It is well known that it was arranged by three Rajas (1) Tungku Chik Penambang (by his Siamese name, Tungku Phra Ahmat) (2) Tungku Petra Dalam Kebun (3) Tungku Sri Mas, or Maharajah."

Chapter 7

Suppressed Evidence: To' Janggut and the Sultan of Kelantan were "Cousins of Sorts"

> ...the Sultan had shut himself up in his palace and was slightly nervous because he heard that the leader of the rebellion was a distant relative of his named To' Janggut.
>
> — Carveth Wells, *Six Years in the Malay Jungle*

Introduction

Although the folk legend links To' Janggut to his feudal lord and indirectly to his pursuit of revenge against the Sultan of Kelantan, it makes no mention that he was related through kinship ties to the Sultan. Yet a British memoir released in 1927 states that the Sultan–To' Janggut relationship was common knowledge in Kota Bahru, and that the Sultan was, in fact, afraid of To' Janggut because he was a *kramat* (a holy man) and invulnerable. Another source, a British government confidential document on Kelantan, goes one step further in its claims about the relationship between the Sultan of Kelantan and To' Janggut. Not only does it state that the two were related, but this source also claims that the Sultan and To' Janggut had been in contact with one another before the rising, and gives the impression that the Sultan was involved in the plot.[1] In this chapter, I shall attempt to explain why the British administration did not publicly reveal the evidence of the Sultan–To' Janggut relationship, and why the folk legend has been silent on this point.

Public Knowledge in 1927

Information about the relationship between the Sultan and To' Janggut emerged in 1927, 12 years after the rebellion, when a former British government official, Carveth Wells, published his book of memoirs, *Six Years in the Malay Jungle*. Wells served as a railway surveyor/district engineer in Pasir Mas (Kelantan) at the time of the rebellion. His account discusses the rumours swirling around Kota Bharu, and states that the Sultan secreted himself up in the palace to avoid To' Janggut. Wells assisted the British troops when they landed at the Pasir Mas beach not far from his residence.

> The numerous *tungkus*, or princes, were very much in evidence, swaggering the streets [of Kota Bharu] in their best clothes, but it was reported that the Sultan had shut himself up in his palace and was slightly nervous because he heard that the leader of the rebellion was a distant relative of his named Tok [sic] Janggut. The name means "an old man with a beard", and he had a beard right down to his knees — but it had only four hairs on it!"
>
> The first news from our "army" was that the police inspector who was in command had met greatly superior forces and had been forced to entrench. We then heard that Tok Janggut had proclaimed himself *kramat* — that is, especially protected by God and invulnerable. To prove it, the old man frequently came out in front of the trenches and allowed the "army" to blaze away at him without effect.
>
> This news which was found to be perfectly true, caused consternation in the Sultan's household, and it was reported that he asked the Adviser to send for assistance.[2]

W. Langham-Carter's Allegations

Wells' account does not implicate the Sultan in the rebellion, but more details about To' Janggut's relationship with the Sultan of Kelantan appear in the British government's confidential files on Kelantan, copies of which are kept in London and in Singapore. In fact, the Sultan's alleged complicity first appears in this confidential official report. However, until recently, the page containing the evidence went missing or was suppressed from the original version of the official report sent to London by the Governor, Sir Arthur Young.

Evidence of a familial relationship between To' Janggut and the Sultan of Kelantan appeared in a 15-page memorandum to the Governor from the British Adviser in Kelantan, W. Langham-Carter.

Curiously, it did not stir Governor Young to order investigations into the matter, or even to ask the Sultan to respond to the allegations. In his official correspondence to London, Young did not evaluate the evidence or draw the attention of the Colonial Office officials to what the British Adviser had said. In fact, his treatment of this "confidential" memorandum was so cavalier that it suggests that he might have hoped that none of the C.O. officials would notice it, and in the event no questions were raised.

One suspects that Langham-Carter's belated revelation greatly embarrassed Young, who had previously sent a report to London approving of the Sultan's conduct and handling of the rebellion, and exonerating the Sultan of any complicity in the disturbance. His despatch was written after a meeting with the Sultan's Malay Ministers in Singapore on 17 May 1915, and Langham-Carter's confidential memorandum, revealing the Sultan's links with To' Janggut, arrived on his desk some three weeks later. It was dated 12 July 1915.

In the copy of Langham-Carter's memorandum sent to the Colonial Office in London, page nine, which reveals the ruler's kinship ties with To' Janggut, is missing. It appears to have been torn out.[3] It is possible that someone in the Colonial Office could have removed the page, but no comments appear on the file folder to indicate this. It is most unlikely that any official in London was involved in a conspiracy with Governor Young to conceal the evidence, and it seems most probable that the page was removed in Singapore. Fortunately, the Governor's original copy of Langham-Carter's memorandum, kept on file at the National Archives in Singapore, is intact and contains the page which is missing in the London copy of the memorandum.

Langham-Carter's memorandum was important in more ways than one. As he was fighting to keep his job, he needed to defend his policies in Kelantan, especially the land tax policy, which had been blamed for the rising at Pasir Putih. To counter criticisms, he had decided to reveal his "trump card" — that the Sultan was secretly in touch with the rebels. He asserted that both To' Janggut and the Sultan were "cousins of sorts" — "*H.H.'s* (His Highness's) *mother was sister to the father or mother of To' Janggut*".[4]

This information had been passed on to him by the British Consul in Trengganu,[5] C.N. Maxwell, brother of W.G. Maxwell, the Governor's Colonial Secretary in Singapore. Langham-Carter also revealed that R.J. Farrer, Governor Young's political intelligence officer, had also obtained certain reports regarding the Sultan's relations with To' Janggut, but he did not say what these were. Langham-Carter said he was unable to verify a rumour that, just before the rising, To' Janggut had sent a letter to the Sultan. He suspected that if the Sultan was interesting himself in the rebels, it was "under cover of Tungku Chik of Penambang", one of the palace officials.

Langham-Carter cast further aspersions on the Sultan's character by stating that the latter was sympathetic to the rebels:

> I venture the personal opinion that the Sultan while desirous by his subscription, messages, etc. of standing well with the British Government as long as it was not decisively worsted has been the whole time at the very least unconvinced of its ultimate success and that so long as he could do so under cover he has been not less than sympathetic with the real rebels whom he now denounces vaguely and with their objects as far as they were disclosed to him. It would be a characteristic attitude at least for a Kelantan Malay.[6]

By implicating the Sultan, Langham-Carter was also forced to reveal that the Sultan was opposed to his policies in Kelantan, especially on land matters.

Langham-Carter's cause was greatly damaged by two earlier official reports submitted to the Governor, which were critical of Langham-Carter's policies and which exonerated the Sultan of complicity in the rebellion. The reports were written by W.G. Maxwell, the Governor's Colonial Secretary, who had been sent to Kota Bahru to investigate the causes of the disturbances, and R.J. Farrer, a political officer also sent by the Governor to accompany the British troops to Kelantan and to report on their role there.

Langham-Carter was clearly disappointed that the other two British officials did not support his view that the Sultan was implicated in To' Janggut's rebellion. While he accepted Farrer's interpretation that the "*tungkus*" or princes, were involved, he commented that the Sultan was not only related to the rebel leader To' Janggut, but was also in league with the "*tungkus*". His statement that "under cover he [the Sultan] has been not less than sympathetic with the real rebels" showed his belief that the Sultan was playing a "double game". By claiming to Langham-Carter and to W.G. Maxwell that the rising was "promoted by those of high estate surrounding him", the Sultan had tried to deflect any implication that he was involved. Although Langham-Carter did not specifically allege that the Sultan, a large-scale landowner, had become involved in the disturbance because of his opposition to the land tax, the British Advisor had no doubt that those of high estate, whoever they were, had been influenced to create a disturbance by the land tax issue.

Farrer Clears the Sultan of Complicity in the Uprising

Farrer's report, dated 31 May 1915, had stated:

> One feature attaching to all the information received at Pasir Putih should be noted, namely the invariable hint that the palace was mixed up in the affair. It was, of course, never a definite suggestion, merely the opinion "if some of the big people did not acquiesce, this could never have happened". I do not think that His Highness the Sultan took any part in fomenting the trouble, (if he did the movement was speedily turned into a channel other than the one he desired), but I cannot avoid a suspicion that some of his entourage was implicated; and the strong attempt made by his emissaries to His Excellency the Governor to throw the blame on Inche Abdul Latif [the District Officer] seems to indicate a desire to find a scapegoat, and to confirm that suspicion. There can be no question but that the chief losers under the new Land Rules will be the Tunkus.[7]

In this respect, Farrer partially agreed with Langham-Carter that the aristocrats were involved, but he cleared the Sultan of any complicity in the rising. Similarly, W.G. Maxwell in his report also said the Sultan had nothing to do with the outbreak. He went on to state that the movement against the land-tax in Pasir Putih, and Ungku Besar's aspirations had the support of certain "Tungkus" of high rank in Kota Bharu. He said, "It is not that His Highness has anything to do with the outbreak.... It is believed — but it is really only a matter for suspicion — that their [the Tungkus'] object was not only to rouse the whole of

Kelantan against the foreigners, as soon as the Pasir Putih outbreak had proved successful, but to depose the Sultan in favour of one of themselves."[8]

Despite the strong case that he put up, it was unfortunate for Langham-Carter that his memorandum arrived too late to influence or change the Governor's mind about his own responsibility for the crisis in Kelantan. In a subsequent chapter, I shall show that the Governor was already convinced that Langham-Carter had partially caused the crisis by introducing the new land rules and taxes without fully explaining them to the people of Pasir Putih. Langham-Carter was subsequently removed as British Adviser and replaced by R.J. Farrer.

Langham-Carter had not only established the Sultan's links with To' Janggut, but with the main players behind the rebellion, that is, "those of high estate". They were opposed to the new land tax, which Langham-Carter had introduced.

Was it, therefore, possible that To' Janggut was one of the "dupes" who had been put up by "those of high estate", including the Sultan, to launch the rebellion?

According to Langham-Carter, Ungku Besar, the feudal lord of Jeram and Pasir Putih districts, had also been part of the plot, as he was himself a big landowner and one of "those of high estate". He had been asked by the British-appointed District Officer to pay land tax, from which he was previously exempt, but had refused. Langham-Carter suspected that Ungku Besar's "pretensions to at least local grandeur and the proximity of Besut [in Trengganu] might have aided the rebels in selecting Pasir Putih, close to the Trengganu border, as the site for their rebellion".

Langham-Carter speculated further, "Besut was at the time of the Pahang war [in 1895–6] a sort of No-man's Land and is still to some extent a sort of modern Alsatis for criminals from Kelantan and Trengganu. In view, however, of the assembly which the Police on the 4th April broke up on the extreme opposite [Trengganu] border of the state I am more than doubtful whether the promoters" activity stopped at Pasir Putih.

> I think indeed that the mere accident of the Sergeant's murder causing the outbreak to take place apparently three days too soon

coupled with Mr Adams' [District Officer's] activity in the Ulu [Kelantan district] saved a much more serious rising, there being evidence that the rebels looked for help from as far away as Pasir Mas, Tanah Merah and the Mersials.

To me it is quite as impossible that the Pasir Putih people had sufficient intelligence to organize unaided a simultaneous rising even of their whole district, whatever else may have been arranged, as it was for anyone to go through the district within some days of the outbreak without realising how completely the whole district had "gone out" — some 200 persons have already been indicated in information as guilty in various degrees.

Nor without previous organisation could the murderers of the sergeant possibly have within an hour or two of the murder poured into Pasir Putih village the numbers that accompanied the first entry, whether they be taken as 100 or 700 or any other figure, 300 being possibly nearly correct.[9]

Unfortunately for Langham-Carter, his memorandum to the Governor, was sidelined, with the crucial page nine missing, and the issue did not get any hearing in the Colonial Office, owing to the precipitate decision of the Governor to support the Sultan's handling of the rebellion. It would have proven a political blunder for Governor Young to reverse his decision and pay attention to what Langham-Carter had said about the Sultan. Fortunately for him, Farrer and Maxwell's reports had also cleared the Sultan of any complicity in the rising.

Nevertheless, Langham-Carter's disclosure of To' Janggut's links with the Sultan and the Sultan's alleged complicity with the rebels creates a real mystery of what the situation really was. It is also a direct challenge to the folk account, which fails to raise the matter. Although the British administration did not publicly mention To' Janggut's alleged links with the Sultan, there was among the people already a suggestion that the palace was mixed up in the affair. Since the kinship tie between To' Janggut and the Sultan was common knowledge in Kota Bharu, it would be odd if the Kelantanese people were not aware of it.

The folk legend's omission of the kinship ties between the Sultan and To' Janggut, and the Sultan's alleged role in the plot behind the rising, may mean that the local folk in Pasir Putih district, from whom much of the *lese-majeste* stories were derived, did not know about these links. But as Carveth Wells had reported, the Sultan–To' Janggut relationship was widely known in Kota Bahru. Wells also said the Sultan was "afraid" of To' Janggut for being a *kramat* and invulnerable. The Sultan might also have been afraid of To' Janggut because of his disguised pursuit of revenge for the murder of his brother by a palace official, which is revealed in the folk account but which Carveth Wells seems unaware of. In any case, since the Sultan had publicly come out to condemn To' Janggut for committing rebellion or *derhaka*, and had ordered the hanging of his corpse in public, an outraged public opinion in Pasir Putih district may have set out to invent a more plausible cause behind To' Janggut's rebellion against the Sultan. As we have seen, the folk account besides projecting To' Janggut as pursuing a personal vendetta, also makes him appear as the dupe of Ungku Besar, but though not of Tungku Chik Penambang and other "Tungkus" of the higher estate, or of the palace, as alleged by the British Adviser. With its implied critique of feudal society and of the Sultan's ultimate role in siding with the British in suppressing the rising, the folk account may have decided simply to transform To' Janggut instead into a nationalistic hero by making him uncompromisingly both anti-British and anti-Sultan.

Chapter 8

Suppressed Photographs and the Imaging of To' Janggut

> In Photography, the presence of the thing (at a certain past moment) is never metaphoric; and in the case of animated beings, their life as well, except in the case of photographing corpses; and even so: if the photograph then becomes horrible, it is because it certifies, so to speak, that the corpse is alive, as *corpse*: it is the living image of a dead thing.
>
> — Roland Barthes, *Camera Lucida* (Vintage, 1993), p. 78

Introduction

The most striking visual image that established To' Janggut's legend was the public display of his corpse. The spectacle, witnessed by thousands of people in Kota Bharu, won him great public support and sympathy. Until recently, the folk account of this incident, as presented by Yahya Abdullah's *Peperangan To' Janggut, atau Balasan Derhaka* and other Kelantanese works has been the major source of the Malaysian public's knowledge about this spectacle. One problem for researchers using this source has been the lack of photographic evidence to verify it.

However, as documented in Chapter 1, Yahya's folk account has been corroborated by three British private sources. One of these sources (Pepys) further reveals that the British administration in Kelantan deliberately suppressed known photographs of the spectacle. Another source (Morkill) retained some photographs of the corpse, thereby defying the government ban but providing researchers with important photographic documentation.

In examining Morkill's photographs, and confronting the visual image of To' Janggut's corpse, it becomes apparent that To' Janggut's visage and other features do not match the physical descriptions of the man that have subsequently emerged within the imagination of the Kelantanese public, in particular, or those of the Malaysian public, in general. This discrepancy reveals the romanticisation of To' Janggut's image in the absence of photographic evidence. This chapter examines the relationship between visual materials and history, and between photographs and memory. Given the elusive and illusionary nature of photography as an art form, we need to ascertain what effect or value these photographic images have on people as images, whether they are superficial objects, possess any "deeper" meanings, and constitute representations of reality.

Photography and Text

Images usually need some explanation. Words are used to ground, situate and pin pictures down or solve them. A (smoker's) pipe in a picture is intractably a pipe, a candy bar a candy bar. But a picture of a corpse or a hanging corpse needs some explanation. Whose corpse is it? How did he die? Where and when did death occur? If it is a gory picture, what reactions do they evoke in a viewer? Who took the picture? Such a specific picture becomes problematic if we lack the knowledge to answer these questions.

Roland Barthes, the French aesthete and philosopher of culture who has studied photography as a language, as a sign, as a spectacle and as theatre, has emphasised the importance of a picture's *referent* but this requires a "secondary action of knowledge or of reflection":

> A specific photograph, in effect is never distinguished from its referent (from what it represents), or at least it is not *immediately* or *generally* distinguished from its referent (as is the case for every other image, encumbered — from the start, and because of its status — by the way in which the object is simulated): it is not impossible to perceive the photographic signifier (certain professionals do so), but it requires a secondary action of knowledge or of reflection.... It is as if the Photograph always carries its referent with itself ... but for there to be a sign there must be a mark; deprived of a principle of marking, photographs are signs which don't *take*, which *turn*, as milk does. Whatever it grants to vision and whatever its manner, a photograph is always invisible: it is not it that we see.'

So what Barthes is saying is that the viewer needs to have the referent of a picture to enable him or her to understand or explain the picture. For instance, a caption which appears on the back of a picture of a hanging corpse and says: "This is the corpse of To' Janggut" certainly helps the viewer. Metaphorically, the subject derives its existence from the photograph, otherwise the photographer has merely embalmed his death in the picture. For Barthes, when he viewed himself in a photograph, he discovered that he had become a "Total-Image, which is to say, Death in person".[2]

Textual and Visual Evidence

One of Morkill's pictures shows a body lying in a bamboo wicker stretcher, and in another it is hanging upside down from a gibbet with the legs tied together. The body (referring to To' Janggut's) was "crucified upside down", recalled W.E. Pepys, the former British District Officer of Pasir Putih who took part in hunting the outlaw.[3]

"It was a stroke of luck that To' Janggut should have been one of the killed, and his death put out any lingering embers of the rising. But he had had the reputation of being invulnerable, and the mere report of his death would not have been believed in Kota Bharu," Pepys said.

"So it was necessary to send his body into the capital, and this was done the same night. On its arrival, the Sultan ordered it to be carried across to the old Execution Ground on the far bank of the Kelantan River, and there to be crucified upside down." Photographs taken at the time were "suppressed and the plates destroyed immediately the Government learned of their existence", said Pepys. "A copy, however, found its way to the London office of *Truth*, which published it and made some caustic comments on the brutal things that were done in the name of the British Empire in the dark corners of the earth. But *Truth* did not know that To' Janggut had been very dead for several days before being hung up there."[4]

Other photographs of the corpse also survived. A few elderly Kelantanese informed me during interviews in Kota Bharu that they had seen a photograph of the corpse of To' Janggut at a *Merdeka* (Independence) Day historical photo exhibition mounted on the wall

The hanging corpse of To' Janggut

This scandalous photograph of the hanging corpse is found in A.G. Morkill's photo album. It could have been taken by him, although he did not caption it. Was a similar photograph of the hanging published in *Truth*? [Copyright Bodleian Library, Oxford (A.G. Morkill collection)] of the state's Information Department in Kota Bharu, the state capital, in 1957 to commemorate Malaya's achievement of independence from colonial rule. Someone had brought his photograph of To' Janggut out from hiding. According to these witnesses, the display at the exhibition celebrated him as a freedom fighter. Public interest in To' Janggut in Kelantan remains undiminished.

In London, although I failed to track down the *Truth* article and photograph, I came across what I believe are surely photographs of To' Janggut. These were found in the photo album of A.G. Morkill, the former British land officer and magistrate, who helped suppress To' Janggut's rebellion. The album is deposited in Oxford at the Rhodes House Memorial Library, which is under the administration of the Bodleian Library of Oxford University. It contains some 20 black and white photographs, probably taken by Morkill himself, and is kept in a cardboard box together with Morkill's hand-written 183-page diary, which provides a week-by-week account of what he did in Kelantan from 25 September 1915 to August 1917.

Unfortunately, neither the diary nor the photo album has any identification or captions for the photographs. This diary encloses a seven-page typed report, which provides some biographical data of Morkill's administrative career and narrates the operations he was involved in against To' Janggut and the other rebels. But he makes no mention of having taken the photographs in his photo album.

In 1984 and again in 1989 I visited Rhodes House Memorial Library to look at Morkill's photo album. On both occasions I felt that the most striking photograph was of a dead body hanging upside down from a gibbet, a goal post-like structure. In another photograph the corpse shows wound marks on the chest and on the right hand. The face is that of a bald old man with a thick wispy beard. His chest is partially clad in a silky white-dotted shirt, while his torso from the waist down is wrapped in a partially rolled up sarong. Although Pepys mentions that he and other British officials had found "unmistakable evidence" of elephantiasis when they lifted the sarong from his body, this information is not apparent in the photograph. Pepys further described To' Janggut's general appearance as follows: "... Of Arab extraction, he had good features and looked, with his eponymous beard, like a character out of the Old Testament. He suffered from elephantiasis, and could walk only with difficulty...."[5]

Morkill's photographs appear to graphically portray the hanging of To' Janggut's corpse, which is vividly described in the Kelantanese folk accounts. However, without identifying captions, can we prove that these images are of To' Janggut? How does one prove or confirm his likeness, particularly when folk accounts have described his body and appearance in heroic, idealised language?

The Ban on the Photographs of To' Janggut

There are a number of reasons why Morkill may have avoided assigning captions to the photographs he took of To' Janggut. If, as Pepys reported, British authorities suppressed photographs taken of the rebel's corpse and destroyed the original plates, Morkill may have feared that he could be accused of retaining banned photographs and defying government orders.

Strangely, the ban was imposed after the authorities had allowed a public display of To' Janggut's corpse in the old Execution yard in front of the former Balai Besar, the Sultan's *istana* (palace). Why, then, were the British authorities in Malaya later so concerned about destroying photographs of To' Janggut's corpse? Perhaps the publication of these photographs in the journal *Truth* made them aware of the potential use of these powerful images to accompany anti-Empirical rhetoric.

In an essay on photography, social critic and writer Susan Sontag has observed that: "photographic images tend to subtract feeling from something we experience at first hand and the feelings they do arouse are, largely, not those we have in real life. Often something disturbs us more in photographed form than it does when we actually experience it."[6]

Sontag recalled that she followed "without queasiness" a three-hour surgical procedure at a hospital in Shanghai in 1973, during which a factory worker had nine-tenths of his stomach removed under acupuncture anesthesia. But when she saw a less gory operation in a documentary film on China, the first cut of the scalpel made her flinch and she averted her eyes several times.

So, the British colonial authorities in Kota Bharu and Singapore apparently flinched, too, and concluded that any photographic image of the hanging of the corpse of To' Janggut could prove damaging to the cause of the British empire in Kelantan.

Still, in the absence of any identification of the photographs in Morkill's album, I regarded the images in the Rhodes House Library largely as items of curiosity only to the few researchers interested in the events of this period.

A Specialist's Reactions

Would the images of a dead (murdered and strung up) body have some meaning for the viewer whether or not the viewer tied the image to a historical knowledge of To' Janggut?

In December 1998, I decided to find out whether the photographs were meaningful to a non-specialist or to a Malaysian, who had grown up with the story of To' Janggut. My former university colleague, Associate Professor Tan Liok Ee, was then at Oxford University doing research at the Rhodes House Library.[7] I thought it was a good opportunity to test a non-specialist's reaction to the photographs.

In my e-mail request to her from Penang I said: "Please do me a favour. Call up this photo album at Rhodes House Library. Tell me what you see and read in the album. I'm curious to find out your reaction." I made no mention at all of To' Janggut. Although it was not specifically her own area of research, I knew she was familiar with research about his rebellion. After viewing the album, she e-mailed back to me: "It was a gory expedition you sent me on. Being a very bad historian, the significance of a diary set in Kelantan 1915 did not hit me immediately and so I was quite unprepared for what awaited me."

"The photo album had no captions at all but the diary contained a hand-written (as well as a type-written version) report by Morkill on the episode. To read the colonial text beside the photos is a lesson in trying to focus one's 'eyes' on 'historical truth'."[8]

Later, in another e-mail she described her reaction more fully:

Of course when a photo album arrives with a record book, rather than read I look at the photo album first. The first few photos show a group of European men, in khaki shorts-type of semi-military uniform in various formations, either practicing marching or preparing for something. After the 6th or 7th photo of the same thing, I was thinking to myself "why is Boon Kheng asking me to look at this!"

Then just as I am getting bored, the next one is suddenly of a man hanging upside down! So I sit up (and immediately my antennae go up and the fact that you have asked me to look at this does help). And the next photo is of a man lying down, dead or sleeping? And then the two photos together — the place, the year and Boon Kheng asking me to look — all come together in a sudden shock.

I realize I am looking at a photo of To' Janggut's corpse — can't remember the lines in Malay, but they come back vaguely about the Sultan ordering his corpse to be displayed in this manner and how this shocked everyone. No mistake when the next photo of the corpse hanging upside down comes up again, and then another one of the corpse, even closer. I immediately opened the book to confirm this, and from the first line of the report, it's confirmed.

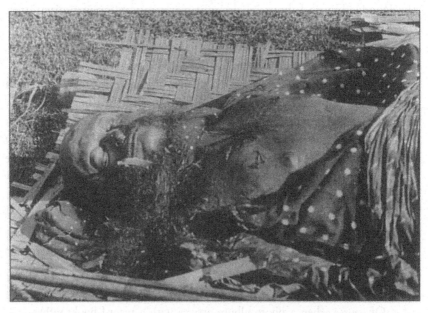

"*... he looked, with his eponymous beard, like a character out of the old Testament....*"
— *Pepys*

[Copyright Bodleian Library, Oxford (A.G. Morkill collection)]

Had there not been the photo of To' Janggut hanging upside down, I wouldn't have been able to identify the close-up of his corpse as there were *no captions* [my emphasis]. What I do want to add to my earlier e-mail was that it [the shock] struck me when I examined the photo of the corpse closely.

After getting over my initial shock when I realised that it was a photo of a dead body (you know what the Chinese are like about dead bodies — you never would photograph them!), I looked at it again and again, realising that I was looking at the face of one of the most controversial figures in Malaysian history.

What struck me was that despite the goriness of the wounds, apparent despite the black and white photo, and the totally disheveled state of the clothing, his face looked peaceful, at rest, and, (not my imagination), almost smiling. Strange in someone who had died such a violent death, bearing all the marks of that death so obviously still on his body. But his eyes were totally closed (always taken as a sign that he was at peace in death. Among the Chinese there is a saying that the

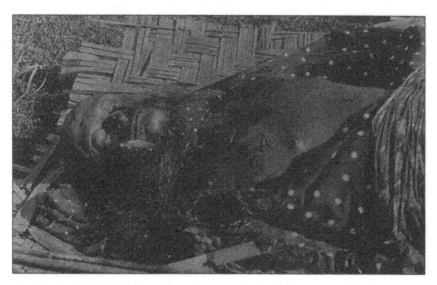

"... *his face looked peaceful, at rest...his eyes were totally closed (but always taken as a sign that he was at peace....)....*" — *Tan Liok Ee*

worst thing to happen to anyone is that they die but cannot close their eyes). I wonder how many died equally violent — or even more violent deaths, whose bodies suffered mutilations, too, but who would never be recognised by you or I in the same way....[9]

Liok Ee succeeded in making an attempt at identification. The fact that the images caused her to be moved, even to be horrified, indicates that the photographic images of To' Janggut do have some meaning to a viewer, do conjure up the violent history of his death. So even without full identification, these images do disturb a viewer's feelings. Although Barthes' point about *referent* is missing here in the case of the Morkill photographs, as Liok Ee's reactions indicate, Barthes' other point is equally valid in that one cannot easily separate the corpse itself as a *corpse* and the violent history the photographic image conjures up even without full knowledge of the rebellion. However, it appears that once the photograph's referent is lost, the object it represents has lost its signifier and its "reality", and it creates a delusion.

> For the photograph's immobility is somehow the result of a perverse confusion between two concepts: the Real and the Live: by attesting that the object has been real, the photograph surreptitiously induces belief that it is alive, because of that delusion which makes us attribute to Reality an absolutely superior, somehow eternal value; but by shifting this reality to the past ("this-has-been"), the photograph suggests that it is already dead.[10]

With its referent long lost and gone, a photograph with no textual or visual evidence for later generations to fall back on is only of a limited value to the curious. However, it may be worthwhile to compare the Morkill photographic images with the "artistic" images of To' Janggut created for present-day viewing. We discover that there is hardly any resemblance at all of one to the other.

Yahya Abdullah's 1955 book, *Peperangan To' Janggut, atau Balasan Derhaka* includes an artist's impression of To' Janggut as an angular faced, handsome, well-groomed man with a white pointed beard and a turban on his head, while the Morkill photographic images show an old man with a round face, bulging eyes, a black wispy beard, and a bald uncovered head.

The artist's attempt to romanticise To' Janggut as an Islamic figure is evident with the turban as his head-dress, as seen in the sketch below.

Sketch taken from Yahya Abdullah, Peperangan To' Janggut, atau Balasan Derhaka (1955)

[Compare this sketch with another romanticised sketch, done 30 years later in a children's story book on To' Janggut, entitled *Pemberontakan Pantai Timor* [Rebellion in the East Coast], written by Rubaidin Siwar and published by Longman's in 1980.]

Tuk Janggut berkempen menentang pemerintahan Inggeris

Sketch from Rubaidin Siwar's Pemberontakan Pantai Timor (1980).

[The caption in Malay reads: "To' Janggut campaigns against the British administration"]

Again, there is a turban, but now, in addition a long beard and flowing robe make To' Janggut look like an Islamic radical. Although historical investigations have not revealed any religious or Islamic factors as underlying causes of the rebellion, local Muslim Malay artists and historians have hinted at such issues in their representation of To' Janggut. In doing so, they have undoubtedly been influenced by the present-day concerns of the international radical Islamic movement. Whether they are historians, writers or artists, the admirers of To' Janggut incorporate present-day issues when they research or look at the past.

Deploring the insertion of present-day concerns into historical interpretation, British historian Professor Richard J. Evans says,

"Historians ... do not just listen to the evidence, they engage in a dialogue with it, actively interrogating it and bringing to bear on it theories and ideas formulated in the present. In this process of dialogue we must be conscious of the nature of these theories and concepts; otherwise, if we abandon our self-consciousness and fail to develop the art of self-criticism to the extent that we imagine we are bringing none, then our prejudices and preconceptions will slip in unnoticed and skew our reading of the evidence...."[11]

Another way of reading the visual evidence, however, is that if the present-day generation of Muslim Malay writers and artists have decided to appropriate the imaging of To' Janggut, it can only mean that his legend is still relevant to them and this relevance, in whatever form or image they decide it should take, merely helps the romance of To' Janggut to live on.

Chapter 9

The Plot Discovered: To' Janggut Launches a Rebellion

An old man named To' Janggut
Turns menacing in a dispute
A policeman killed he
Making all hell break loose

*   *   *

In the ceaseless din and uproar
To' Janggut urged defiance and revolt
People joined him in large numbers
Ready to be killed or wounded

*   *   *

Tungku Besar Cerang the reported rebels' ringleader
Plotted a long while ago to bring about this trouble
Seeking first alliance with one and then all
To seize Kelantan for himself.[1]

Introduction

The first week of the rising was extremely chaotic and events were seen differently by the British officials and the palace in Kota Bahru. British officials stated publicly in the newspapers that the rising was over land-taxes. But within official circles in Kelantan a discourse occurred over whether the rising was a "personal war" by To' Janggut, or something orchestrated by Ungku Besar and other aristocrats who were large land-owners, with or without the support of the Sultan. This official discourse, found only in once-classified files of the British government that are now located in Kota Bahru, Singapore and London, raised questions over whether To' Janggut's unpremeditated act in killing the police sergeant had refocused the rebellion in ways that were not originally intended. In his actions, To' Janggut put his personal stamp on the rebellion. Whether or not To' Janggut was a leader of the rebellion or was manipulated into following the wishes of other dissatisfied leaders, he appears to have been motivated by a hidden agenda, and the rebellion might still seem like a "personal war". All accounts indicate that because of his violent temper To' Janggut was not easily controlled, and that fact certainly played out in the events of the rebellion as they unfolded.

The Controversy

Although To' Janggut and Ungku Besar initially became the best-known figures in the rebellion at Pasir Putih, it now transpires that the British authorities did not think that they were the true instigators of the rebellion. Although records show that To' Janggut's murder of the police sergeant on 29 April 1915 did officially start the rebellion, records reveal that according to British intelligence the first attack of the rebellion was planned for a few days later. To' Janggut's violent action was the spontaneous action of an impetuous, irascible individual. To this extent, the Kelantanese folk legend is right in calling his action *Musuh To' Janggut* or *Peperangan To' Janggut* — "To' Janggut's Rebellion". But there is evidence to suggest that bigger forces were behind the planning of the rebellion.

Controversy raged among the British officials on the origins of the rising, especially on how best to interpret the events that led to the murder of the sergeant. British Adviser, W. Langham-Carter, thought the killing of the sergeant was unpremeditated, but believed there was a plot and that the large aristocratic land-owners had set To' Janggut up as a dupe in their efforts to oppose the new land tax. He believed that the ultimate aim of the rebellion was to overthrow the government and drive out foreigners. British official, R.J. Farrer, agreed with this reading of events, and dismissed the interpretation provided by a Dato Setia, the Malay plenipotentiary of the Sultan that the rising was merely a protest by To' Janggut and the peasants against the tax-collecting methods of the District Officer, Abdul Latiff.

The Suspected Ringleaders

As we have seen in Chapter 5, a group of aristocratic major land-owners, who were unhappy with the prospect of paying land-taxes was identified by British authorities as the instigators of the Pasir Putih rising. Cleverly concealed themselves behind the scenes, these aristocrats could not remain hidden indefinitely because a wide range of sources, including government officers, police informers, captured rebels and ordinary peasants, helped reveal their involvement. However, the British authorities hesitated in taking action against these suspected ringleaders, in large part because the evidence was not sufficiently incriminating.

Besides advancing their own claims and grievances against the new land tax, the aristocrats appear to have adopted the strategy of encouraging their peasant supporters to promote a variety of different causes to distract attention from themselves. These included dissatisfaction with the new land taxes, Ungku Besar's desire to be a Raja, peasant dislike of foreigners (*orang luar*), and opposition to the Singapore-born District Officer, Abdul Latif, along with his tax-collecting clerks, the Sikh police and the British officials.

Because, no British official ever issued a public statement accusing the large land-owners of any involvement in the rebellion, evidence of their participation emerged only when the confidential government files of British officials in Kelantan, Singapore and London were finally opened and available to researchers.

The most important information about the instigators of the rebellion came from the largest landholder himself, the Sultan of Kelantan. He owned 3,000 acres of land, on which the British Adviser, W. Langham-Carter, had insisted that he pay assessment and land-taxes. The ruler unhappily agreed to pay when it was decided that "a number of people of position who have hitherto evaded payment of any tax" had to be put on the rent rolls, said R.F. Farrer, who added, "It must be borne in mind, too, that some of the members of the Royal Family have in the past been practically exempt from payment of the produce taxes, and that they realize that the new rules will put an end to this state of things."[2] In his diary, Morkill narrates attempts by the Sultan and other royals to interfere with his survey and assignment of land for smallholdings. He was frequently involved in wrangles with the Sultan about new settlements over land claimed by the ruler as his own.[3] The Sultan, however, confided in Langham-Carter and in other British officials in Kelantan that he suspected his relations, many of them large landowners like himself, were behind the rising, but he refused to disclose their names.

The British Adviser suspected that the Sultan's two uncles, Tungku Besar and Tungku Bendahara, and another member of royalty, Tungku Chik Penambang, were involved. Langham-Carter came across their names during his investigation into the causes of the rebellion, and he thought these aristocrats were not only opposing the new land tax, but also intending to depose the Sultan "in favour of one of themselves". W.G. Maxwell, the Colonial Secretary in Singapore sent by the Governor to investigate the causes of the rebellion, reported the suspicions of the Sultan and the British Adviser as follows:

> The movement against the land-tax in Pasir Putih, and Engku [sic] Besar's aspirations had the support of certain "Tungkus" [sic] of high rank in Kota Bahru. His Highness the Sultan told me he was certain of this. He would not give me any names, as he was still making enquiries. I may say, however, the persons suspected by the British Adviser are the Tungku Besar, the Tungku Bendahara, and Tungku Chik Penambang. All three are members of the State Council. It is believed — but it is really only a matter for suspicion — that their object was not only to arouse the whole of Kelantan against the foreigners, as soon as the Pasir Putih outbreak had proved successful, but to depose the Sultan in favour of one of themselves.[4]

The District Officer of Pasir Putih, Abdul Latif, however, alleged that Tungku Chik Penambang engineered the rebellion with the avowed object of becoming Sultan himself.[5] According to Langham-Carter, the Sultan expressed similar fears about his uncle Tungku Besar, but Langham-Carter also shared the suspicions of Maxwell against Tungku Chik Penambang, Tungku Petra Dalam Kebun, Sri Maharaja and the Datoh Mentri, the Sultan's Minister:

> The Tungkus have still a large and somewhat sinister influence in the country, and this will most likely prevent proof positive of which of them, and to what extent they were responsible for the

rising. They and their class would have been the losers by any
system in which dues must inevitably be paid and that alone would
suffice to account for any promotion of disturbance by them, for
all would hope to improve their position by it. In addition to His
Highness' suspicions, there is third hard [sic] or weaker evidence
against various Tungkus and in particular against Tungku Chik of
Penambang and Sri Maharaja, and also against the Datoh Mentri.
Against Tungku Besar, however, the Sultan's own suspicions are
plainly directed.... Assuming that all started with the avowed
object of getting rid of the land tax and of generally bettering their
position it is not impossible that each of the first three had wider
secret ambitions which they hoped to realise if the non-Kelantanese
could be driven out. Each has some kind of claim to the Throne
and it is one of the unprovable allegations that Tungku Chik had
a promise of support in his from Tungku Petra Dalam Kebun,
himself rather a strong claimant, but resident himself habitually
in Siamese territory. There is evidence also that his representative
in land matters in Pasir Putih was taking a prominent part in
the rising.[6]

To Langham-Carter and to several other British officials, the most
telling evidence came from members of the public in Pasir Putih, who
also revealed the involvement of the Tungkus. The man whose name
kept coming up in the interviews was Tungku Chik Penambang.[7]

For instance, Che Mat, a chief clerk at the District Office in
Pasir Putih, declared to W.E. Pepys, the District Officer: "When I was
going to Kota Bahru from Pasir Putih after the (first) attack, I met near
Gunong some men who asked me whether it was true Pasir Putih was
sacked. They said, 'This is not the people's doing. It is well known that
it was arranged by three Rajas (1) Tungku Chik Penambang (by his
Siamese name, Tungku Phra Ahmat) (2) Tungku Petra Dalam Kebun,
and (3) Tungku Sri Mas, or Maharajah.'"[8]

Tungku Chik Penambang was also identified as a ringleader by
two other members of the public, Dolah Timun and H. Daud.

If these allegations are correct, it clearly suited the interests of
the aristocrats that To' Janggut's reputation as a fearless fighter should
spread widely throughout Kelantan, so that, by contrast, their own
involvement in the rebellion might not become noticeable. By publicly
refusing to pay taxes and by committing the murder, To' Janggut took

the initiative and boldly defied the authorities in both Pasir Putih town and in Kota Bahru. By the third week, he and the other rebel chiefs had been publicly named and declared outlaws by the Sultan of Kelantan. Each carried a prize of $500 on his head. But the identity of the principals remained concealed:

> Whereas the under-mentioned persons, namely, Ungku Besar of Jeram, Haji Md. Hassan (alias To' Janggut) of Nering, Penghulu Adam of Kelubi, Haji Sahid of Cherong Tuli and Che Sahak of Nering were on the 12th May last given by H.H. the Sultan of Kelantan seven days in which to surrender and answer various matters alleged against them
>
> And whereas such persons have not surrendered and have not answered the charges against them H.H. the Sultan now desires to make known that he will give a reward of $500 to whomsoever shall bring in any one of the persons above-named dead or alive.[9]

The official list shows To' Janggut's standing in the rebel party as No. 2, but in the eyes of the Kelantan *ra'yaat* he was also the "invulnerable" military leader. His murder of the police sergeant gave him notoriety among the Kelantan folk, but Langham-Carter concluded that the murder was a "mere accident ... causing the outbreak to take place apparently three days too soon".[10] He said that the "rebels looked for help from as far away as Pasir Mas, Tanah Merah and the Kersial", but Pasir Mas District Officer Adams' activity in organising resistance "saved a much more serious rising". Langham-Carter claimed that about a month before the rising, the Sultan had called him and the Superintendent of Lands to a meeting of Tungkus, who attacked the new land-rent system. "There can, however, have been left in the minds of the meeting no doubt as to whether the system would be adhered to, and I personally am certain that from that time those who stood to lose by its advantages improperly enjoyed under the produce tax system set in active motion the Pasir Putih dupes," he wrote. "Without some certainty as to who were the leading spirits in Kota Bahru, I cannot say why this district was selected unless because it was geographically and otherwise somewhat more out of control or contained people the majority of whom were rather more stupid than other parts of Kelantan."[11]

The Events of the Rebellion

The Unpremeditated Murder: Three Different Versions

The folk account, *Peperangan To' Janggut, atau Balasan Derhaka*, identifies the five ringleaders of the rebellion as Ungku Besar, To' Janggut, Penghulu Adam, Haji Said and Enche Ishak. Besides the first named, the others were merely padi cultivators. The account traced the rising to Ungku Besar's desire to become the ruler of Pasir Putih, and clearly shows how he instigated To' Janggut and others to join him in refusing to pay taxes.

In telling To' Janggut's story, the folk account gives the impression that he might have been induced also to seek revenge for the death of his father, or the death of his old brother at the hands of a henchman of the Sultan of Kelantan. But it treats his murder of the police sergeant, who had been sent by the District Officer to investigate social disturbances among the villagers, as an unpremeditated incident and that a hot-tempered To' Janggut had spontaneously transformed the rebellion into his "personal war".

According to the folk version, when the sergeant attempted to bring To' Janggut and others to court to face charges of not paying taxes, he provoked To' Janggut by asking him to walk in front. To' Janggut refused, saying, "I will not walk in front of you because it will mean that I am guilty and am your prisoner." In the heat of the moment, To' Janggut drew his *keris* and stabbed the sergeant. As the man fell, he was set upon by To' Janggut's followers.

There are two variant versions of this incident that marks the beginning of To' Janggut's "personal war".

The version of the incident given by Dato Setia and Dato Menteri, the two Malay officials sent by the Sultan to meet with the Governor in Singapore has the sergeant killed when he attempts to handcuff To' Janggut:

> ... On the Sergeant's arrival at To' Janggut's house, he was informed by the owners that he did not refuse to pay the tax but he had no money to pay it with. The Sergeant informed him that he must go and see the District Officer at Pasir Putih. To' Janggut, who was an old man, obeyed but walked very

slowly and the Sergeant thereupon ordered a policeman to bring a pair of handcuffs. On these being brought he proceeded to handcuff To' Janggut who drew his *kris* and stabbed him. Whilst struggling with him he was stabbed in the back by a relation of To' Janggut. This stab caused the death of the Sergeant.[12]

A third version — given by W.G. Maxwell, a British official[13] — reveals that a plot for an intended attack on the District Office had been discovered a day earlier, and that To' Janggut, on learning that the authorities were now aware of their plot, had decided to pre-empt matters with his killing of the sergeant:

> On the evening of Wednesday 28th April, the District Officer was warned by the headman of the district of Jeram that the men of the various villages in his district had decided not to pay any taxes. The villagers had gathered at a particular place to discuss an attack upon Pasir Putih town with the object of driving out the Government officials. On the following morning (29 April), the police sergeant, Che Wan, with a police constable and a detective, proceeded to Jeram to make enquiries.
>
> In the first few villages, they learnt nothing. Later, in the village of Merbul, they came upon a collection of about twenty people. The villagers said they were discussing the matter of a stolen buffalo. The sergeant took all their names, and then ordered them to accompany him to see the district officer. After some expostulation, they obeyed, but before they had gone more than a few yards, a man named Haji Mat Hassan — better known as To' Janggut (Old Long Beard) — attacked the sergeant with a kris, and after a struggle, in which others assisted him, succeeded in stabbing the sergeant to death.[14]

These different versions agree that an impetuous To' Janggut "started" the rebellion by stabbing the sergeant, causing his death. Initially, even the Governor had received a slightly different version of who had murdered the police sergeant.[15] The actual context in which the stabbing occurred, however, is open to various interpretations. But the probability of To' Janggut's unpremeditated action is clear. So is that of a *planned revolt* as the Kelantanese folk account and Maxwell's published account coincide and confirm one another.

Three Days Too Early

R.J. Farrer, the Governor's political agent who accompanied the British expeditionary force into Pasir Putih, also asserted that the real reason for the murder was that the sergeant had gone to enquire about the large gathering and the probability of an attack on Pasir Putih. "The murder of the sergeant by To' Janggut merely precipitated matters by a few days," observed Farrer. "I do not believe Dato Stia's account of the murder. The sergeant was sent to enquire the reason for the assembling of some 40 men at To' Janggut's house, and as to the probability of an attack being made on Pasir Putih. It is inconceivable that a Malay sergeant, accompanied by one constable would use violence to a man of To' Janggut's reputation in the presence of a number of that man's supporters."[16]

Farrer in his report also disclosed that there were two attacks on Pasir Putih town after the sergeant's murder. In the first, the land office and police station were ransacked, and some private houses pillaged; while in the second two days later, some private houses were burnt — "it is believed in order to create confusion and facilitate the sack of the rest of the shops — as a good deal of property had been removed in the meantime".[17]

Maxwell's report reveals that although the outbreak occurred in Pasir Putih district, there was clear evidence that messages were sent by Ungku Besar and To' Janggut to various people in other parts of the state urging them to stage a simultaneous rising.[18] "The Malays of the other districts, however, were only waiting to see the result of the movement in Pasir Putih," wrote Maxwell in his confidential report to the Governor. "When Colonel Brownlow's force and H.M.S. 'Cadmus' arrived, the Malays of Kota Bharu district threw in their lot with them and with the Government. If that military and naval force had not been sent from Singapore, the Sultan would have got no response to his forced levy."

The rising began with To' Janggut and some hundreds of Malays advancing to attack Pasir Putih town. "It is beyond doubt that the people of Pasir Putih district, as a whole, were practically united in their sympathy with the rioters," wrote Maxwell. The District Officer sent messages for help to the nearest villages, Gal and Ko'Brangan, but the reply came that they were on To' Janggut's side and would render no assistance.

Although he considered that the killing of the sergeant was unpremeditated, the British Adviser, W. Langham-Carter speculated that it had, in fact, averted a larger general rising. "I think indeed that the mere accident of the Sergeant's murder causing the outbreak to take place apparently three days too soon coupled with Mr Adams' [District Officer's] activity in the Ulu [Kelantan district] saved a much more serious rising, there being evidence that the rebels looked for help from as far away as Pasir Mas, Tanah Merah and the Kersials.... Nor without previous organisation could the murderers of the sergeant possibly have within an hour or two of the murder poured into Pasir Putih village the numbers that accompanied the first entry, whether they be taken as 100 or 700 or any other figure, 300 being possibly nearly correct," he stated, in some astonishment, asking how To' Janggut was able to call out such large numbers of people so quickly.[19]

Immediately after the district officer's departure from Pasir Putih, the police divested themselves of their uniforms, says Maxwell's report. They and all the clerks and other officials either hid or ran away. At about 4.00 p.m., To' Janggut's party arrived in the town, shouting and yelling. One account put them at about a hundred in number. But several hundred Malays came in from the neighbouring villages to lend support and to take part in the pillaging. Armed with lances, hatchets, keris and axes, they called upon the district officer and the land officer clerk by name to come out and collect their land tax, and then proceeded to loot the police station and government offices and to destroy the records.

The prisoners in the lock-up were set free. The cattle taken from the pound were butchered for food. Three or four other native shops were looted, and three Malay shophouses near the district officer's quarters were burnt to the ground, whether by accident or design is not clear, but no government buildings were destroyed. "A local chief Engku Besar took a leading part in the crowd of rioters," says Maxwell's report, "and it is believed that he hoped to follow up the expulsion of the government officials by setting himself up in Pasir Putih as an independent ruler".[20]

How To' Janggut and Ungku Besar Led the Attack on the Prison

After the murder of the police sergeant, To' Janggut led the attack on Pasir Putih town, especially the police station. Magistrate court records provide eye-witness accounts from several accused persons and prisoners who took part in the activities.

At the police station To' Janggut recruited the freed prisoners' support, and seized police weapons. Some prisoners later claimed that they had been threatened with violence if they refused to join the rebels. To' Janggut's followers included a number of locally known criminals, who the town's residents recognised. They informed the police who subsequently arrested these men.

Awang bin Awang, one of the prisoners released from Pasir Putih gaol, gave this account of what took place:

> The crowd in the police station broke open the safe, and tore up the books and seized arms, rifles from the back and confiscated guns from the store. Awang Hat and two others broke up the lock-up with an axe. He said, "*Lock-up ini sombong sangat sudah masuk saya*" ("This lock-up is resisting, but I have entered it."). When they had finished, Awang Hat bade me leave and said, "If you don't, you will starve. All government men have bolted." So then they went away. I came out and Tok Janggut bade me follow him. I met him on the road in Pasir Putih. He said he would stab me if I would not follow him. So I followed him up to Ulu Kalubi. When his followers were massed there I asked leave to go home, and he allowed me to, but bade me come again next day....[21]

The rebels also asked another prisoner, Awang Hamat bin Seludin, to join them:

> I was in gaol when To' Janggut came to Pasir Putih. I had been there 50 days, on a three-month sentence, together with Awang bin Awang. Some 400 men came in to the police station....To' Janggut himself did not enter.... They broke up the police station. Awang Hat cut the bars of the gaol with an axe...I came out and was made to follow To' Janggut, but I got permission to go home....[22]

A padi planter named Brahim bin Botok joined the rebels the day after the sergeant's death (that is, on 30 April). He too claimed to have been threatened.

> ... I came to Pasir Putih about 8 a.m., being ordered to do so by Ungku Besar. This I heard from a lot of people. I heard gongs and they said Ungku Besar bade us go to Pasir Putih, or our own houses would be burnt down. About 300 of us went down.... We were told that our houses would be burnt down and cattle stolen if we didn't go to Pasir Putih, and so we came. We assembled at the house of Awang Osman at the entrance to the town. There we heard our orders were to burn everything and destroy all of no value, taking what was of value, and also to run amok among the *orang luar* (foreigners). The Ungku Besar himself ordered us to do this at 3 p.m. on either the Saturday or Sunday following the sergeant's death. I had a kris with me.... My orders were to fight the police and government servants, because taxes were so unjust in To' Janggut's opinion. This was an order from Ungku Besar and To' Janggut.... I and the followers of Ungku Besar were like sheep or chicken, merely following our leader, without using thought for ourselves.[23]

The situation in Pasir Putih was so fluid that many people were forced to change sides quickly. First they became rebels, then government supporters. In fact, when the British troops arrived in Pasir Putih, shopkeepers who had returned to the town on hearing of their approach asked why they had brought with them "so many of the men who had taken part in looting their shops".[24] Those who committed thefts and used violence on others were not let off easily, as their victims remembered their faces and reported their names to the authorities.

The case of Haji Awang Ngah bin Mamat, a rice farmer, highlighted the "double role" some people played. Pasir Putih residents recognised him as one of the leaders of the rebel mob, walking with them back and forth through the town, but in his defence he claimed he was acting as "a detective" for the *Tok Kweng* (penghulu or village chief) and pretending to be a rebel. He surrendered himself to the police when he discovered that he was on their "wanted" list, and gave the following statement.

> I have nothing to do with Tungku Chik. I merely work his padi. I am in a way his *wakil* (agent), but not by virtue of any written authority. In the latter sense Haji Wan Daud is his *wakil*. I have never held a written *kuasa* (authority) from Tungku Chik Penambang, though I have received a book in which to receive

rents. I have so worked a long time, nearly 10 years. All his land is *pesaka* (inheritance). He has bought none, nor taken any.[25]

Although the man's links with Tungku Chik Penambang were clearly established, the authorities could learn nothing further from him about the aristocrat's involvement in rebel activities.

Conclusion

If the rising was indeed orchestrated from behind the scene, were the ringleaders content with the direction events had taken? As Langham-Carter speculated, it seems likely that To' Janggut's accidental killing of the police sergeant caused the rising to take a different direction from what had been intended, thereby averting a more general rising. Whatever the original aims of the rebellion were, once the killing took place, To' Janggut took on a role as the agent of change and leader of the rebellion. The rising became his story and he would forever be tied to it in the minds of the public.

Chapter 10

The Sultan's Double Game

> I venture the personal opinion that the Sultan while desirous by his subscription, messages, etc. of standing well with the British Government as long as it was not decisively worsted has been the whole time at the very least unconvinced of its ultimate success and that so long as he could do so under cover he has been not less than sympathetic with the real rebels whom he now denounces vaguely and with their objects as far as they were disclosed to him. It would be a characteristic attitude at least for a Kelantan Malay.
>
> — W. Langham-Carter, British Adviser of Kelantan in his original "unexpurgated" memorandum to the Governor, 12 July 1915

Introduction

W. Langham-Carter accused the Sultan of Kelantan of being duplicitous in his stand on the rising, of playing a "double game". It was a serious charge to level at him. Apparently, because Langham-Carter's memorandum reached the Governor only after he had approved of the Sultan's conduct and exonerated him of any involvement in the rising, no action was taken against the Sultan. Moreover, as previously stated, the copy received by the Colonial Office in London had the incriminating page removed.

In this chapter, I intend to show that Langham-Carter's allegations were not unfounded. Although he did not prove his case in his memorandum, there is substantial evidence in the British administration records in Kelantan and Singapore to support the notion that the Sultan was, indeed, playing a double game. Apparently some awareness or recollection of this emerged later among British officials in London and Trengganu years later, when the Trengganu disturbances of 1922, 1925 and 1928 triggered a comparison was made between those events and the Kelantan disturbances.

In this account, I intend to show that Langham-Carter and the Sultan had experienced serious disagreements over the causes of the rising, worsening a relationship that had already become difficult even before the rising. In his book *Rulers and Residents*, John Gullick has shown that such conflicts between Malay rulers and British Residents/Advisers were quite common in British Malaya.[1]

Although there are few examples of the Sultan's speech or writing, numerous British documents in the Colonial Office records report his words. In fact, owing to the availability of such evidence in London and in the files of the British Adviser for Kelantan held in the National Archives of Malaysia, the conflict between the Sultan and the British Adviser can be studied in depth. These sources further reveal the Sultan's sympathetic stand towards the rebels, his duplicity during the rising, and how he was able to manipulate events in order to oust Langham-Carter. This picture of the Sultan is different from that of the pliant, pro-British individual portrayed in folk accounts of the rebellion. Furthermore, it shows that the rising generated serious dissension and conflict within the top circles of administration in Kelantan.

The Sultan-Adviser Conflict

From the moment the rebellion became known in Kota Bahru, a misunderstanding developed between the Sultan and Langham-Carter over how to respond. The Sultan initially attempted to use his own local forces or levies but later advocated settling the issue through negotiations, but the British Adviser wanted a quick military solution and immediately summoned military assistance from Singapore. The British Adviser would later be reprimanded for requesting troops. W.E. Pepys says: "He [Langham-Carter] was criticised for having called for assistance from Singapore to suppress the Rising — unfairly in my opinion."[2] The Governor in a report to the Colonial Office revealed that he had received telegrams on 1 and 2 May from the British Adviser informing him of the rebellion and requesting troops:

The Sultan, the Adviser stated, undertook to deal with the situation, but in case he was unable to do so, he (the Adviser) would telegraph and, on his so doing, he hoped the 200 Regulars would be sent. The number of those who had risen was not known but a report stated that it did not exceed 5,000. On the morning of the 2nd May, a further telegram was received merely saying, "Send as soon as possible help...."[3]

The Sultan

Initial reports from British officials in Kelantan accuse the Sultan of minimising the seriousness of the rebellion. He was reluctant to use the British forces sent from Singapore, although initially he preferred to use his own Malay officials and armed levies to meet the rebels. The Adviser agreed to his plan on the condition that the Sultan's forces only attempt to deal with the rebellion before the arrival of British troops, and thereafter give their full cooperation to British forces. Both the British Adviser and the political (intelligence) officer attached to the Army, R.J. Farrer, were immediately suspicious of the Sultan's intentions. The Sultan and Langham-Carter also disagreed on other issues that developed in the course of the military expedition to suppress the rebels, and a degree of ambivalence over the Sultan's actions and reported statements fed the suspicions of Farrer and Langham-Carter.

Farrer, who accompanied the British force that arrived in Kelantan on 5 May, explained his suspicions of the Sultan in a report dated 31 May:

H.H. the Sultan, on whom Colonel Brownlow and I called after arriving at Kota Bahru, minimised the matter, and declared that he could deal with his own forces with the 100 or so rebels, which, he said, were all these were. He was clearly very nervous, and very anxious that Colonel Brownlow's force should remain inactive. Three members of his Council, obviously called in to strengthen his position, supported him. The Adviser pointed out that previous events had shown the groundlessness of His Highness's confidence, and suggested that his forces should cooperate with the British troops if they should not have proved successful before the British force arrived at the scene of disturbance.[4]

This meeting took place on 5 May, a week after the outbreak. But how had previous events "shown the groundlessness of His Highness's confidence"? Apparently, between 29 April and 5 May two rumours had caused the British Adviser to regard the situation in Kelantan as serious, leading him to request military assistance.[5]

A newspaper account written by an anonymous writer (later revealed to be W.G. Maxwell) and published on 29 May, a week after the rebellion had been quelled, describes these two rumours and detailed the actions taken by the Sultan and the British Adviser:

> Early on the morning of the 30th [April], the British Adviser had an interview with H.H. the Sultan, who decided to collect by forced labour a body of the peasants living near Kota Bahru and to send them under their headmen and officials to oppose the rioters. By this time it was stated upon apparently good authority, and generally believed, that a body of five thousand men from Pasir Putih was advancing on Kota Bahru. (It is now known that the rioters made no attempt to move towards Kota Bahru. They were merely collected at Ungku Besar's house in Jeram village). There was also a rumour, which was wholly untrue, that two elephant loads of ammunition had been sent to the rioters from Trengganu. In addition to raising this levy, His Highness decided to send two of his ministers, Datoh Setia and Dato Mentri, to parley with the rioters. The guards in Kota Bahru were doubled, and pickets of special constables were posted at various places.[6]

The Sultan's levies failed to stop the rebels and arrest their leaders and rumours of further rebel activity caused considerable anxiety. On 6 May suspicion had fallen on the Sultan's men, in particular the Sultan's minister, Dato Setia, who by 3 May had returned from negotiations with the rebels and communicated to both the Sultan and the British Adviser their demand for a full pardon, which the Sultan rejected. The British Adviser questioned how the Sultan could be so confident and "minimize" the matter on 5 May, when tensions in the capital had risen and the Sultan had intensified security around his palace amidst rumours of an impending attack. On the same day further suspicions that the Sultan was trying to delay the British force were raised by "contradictory" information again given by Dato Setia after the British force's arrival in Gunong. These suspicions are clearly expressed in Farrer's confidential report of 31 May:

After the arrival of the force at Gunong on May 6th, the Dato
Setia arrived with much detailed information regarding the
numbers, dispositions, and plans of the rebels. This information
was so precise that it occurred both to the Adviser and myself that
it might have been concocted in order to further His Highness's
policy of preventing action by the British troops. On the 7th the
Dato Setia's information had reverted to that given by the Sultan
on the 5th.[7]

*This photograph believed to be that of the troops of the Malay States Guides,
comprising Sikhs and Malays, who were standing in the rear, while their British
officers stand in the front line. They had marched from Kota Bharu to a site near
Pasir Putih to hunt for the rebels.*

[Copyright Bodleian Library, Oxford (A.G. Morkill collection)]

Maxwell's newspaper report describes the same events but omits
the suspicions articulated in Farrer's report. It treats the rumours that
delayed the advance of the British forces as strategic problems, which
any military expedition might encounter. The British forces paid proper
heed to the rumours, as Maxwell observed:

During this time, [Chief Police Inspector] Jackson's force remained in the vicinity of Gunong without seeing any sign of the rioters. The information of their presence, in number of three to five thousand men between Gunong and Pasir Puteh was, however, so definite and circumstantial that it was not considered possible to advance against them.

On May 6th, Colonel Brownlow sent a detachment of 50 Europeans and the Malay Volunteers to Tanah Merah, a village on the railway line, where trouble was expected, and proceeded with the remainder of his force to Gunong, where he halted.

At Gunong, the information of the presence of the rioters in large numbers, was so circumstantial in all particulars and came from sources, apparently so well informed, that Colonel Brownlow decided to send for the detachment at Tanah Merah. This arrived on 7 May, and on 8 May the whole force advanced to Solising, a distance of about 7½ miles, progress being delayed by the difficulties of the transport of bullock carts and two maxim guns across the padi-fields.[8]

Farrer had a different explanation for the delay. Although the British force did not encounter the rebels, he said, their march to Pasir Putih between 8 and 9 May had encountered delaying tactics employed by the Kelantanese population, the Malay coolies, the Dato Setia and the Sultan's levies which made their passage difficult. Farrer presented these problems in his report of 31 May as follows:

The advance from Gunong to Pasir Puteh (8th and 9th May) was uneventful. The demeanour of the inhabitants of Selising [sic], where we stopped the night of the 8th was not friendly, and on the 9th the coolies collected on the way by the Adviser to take the place of rikisha transport when that broke down, refused to proceed after traveling about one and a half miles on the pretext that they were approaching the boundaries of another headman's district, and my appeal to the Dato Setia and Tungku Muda (who were near by) for an order to them to proceed resulted in the substitution of a fresh lot of coolies after some delay.

On the 9th we saw practically for the first time the Sultan's "*levee en masse*". It consisted of picturesque cohorts of men of many ages armed with throwing spears and *krises* and *parangs*, whose uniform was a band of red stuff tied round one arm. On our arrival at Pasir Puteh various shopkeepers, who had returned to the village on hearing of our approach, were curious as to why we had brought with us so many of the men who had taken part in looting their shops.[9]

Surprisingly, however, the Army's report omitted many of these points. Col. Brownlow, in a report of 16 May that was sent separately to military headquarters in Singapore, simply described some of the problems encountered by his force. One of these was rumours, which apparently had genuinely played havoc with the military expedition. Col. Brownlow, however, affirmed Farrer's opinion about the Sultan's lack of enthusiasm. On 5 May, he reported, he and Langham-Carter had called on the Sultan, "who appeared unwilling that the force should march, but no change of plans was made".[10] At 6 a.m. the following day a report was received that the police station at Tanah Merah had been attacked during the night. Col. Brownlow decided to leave with a force and headed for Gunong. A short distance from Gunong, he met Chief Inspector Jackson of the Kelantan Police Force, who told him that a large force of rebels was marching on Kota Bahru via Gunong. Brownlow's force accordingly pushed on to a point about 1¾ miles south of Gunong with a view to laying an ambush, but he then learned that the report was not true. The troops then bivouacked in the grounds of the Sultan's house in Gunong.

Sultan Mohamed IV of Kelantan (reign 1902–20) taken in 1909

[Copyright National Archives of Malaysia, Kuala Lumpur]

On the role played by Dato Setia, Col. Brownlow reported, "the Dato Setia, private secretary to the Sultan, came and gave me the following information regarding the enemy:

> They are disposed as follows (given on rough map):

At Bukit Abar (3 miles south of Bukit Jawa)	200 men
At Padang Pa'amat (2 miles S.E.of Bukit Abar)	1,000 men
About ½ a mile E. of Bukit Abar	200 men
On path Bukit Abar to Padang Pa'mat not more than 1 mile from road	300 men
West of path to Pasir Puteh, about opposite to Padang Pa'amat	200 men
At Wakaf Berangan, 2 miles N. of Pasir Puteh main body	2,000 men
Total	3,900 men

> There are about 400 guns with this force of which 150 are muzzle loaders, the remainder being breech loading rifles. The enemy's plan is that the force at Bukit Abar should act as a bait and that when we attack it the forces on all sides shall attack our flanks and the main body shall come up to attack our front. This information agreed with that already given by Mr Jackson and I was advised by Mr Langham Carter that I should attach importance to it."[11]

If the Sultan's intention was to obstruct the movement of the British force, he could not prevent it finally from reaching its destination. Was the delay then to give more time to the rebels to redeploy themselves before the arrival of the British troops? Assuming that this was his strategy, he also had to vary his strategy quickly to show support for other British actions, otherwise suspicions would emerge on the British side that he was opposing use of the troops and showing support for the rebels, as such suspicions were to appear later in the report of Farrer.

The Sultan's Version

On 17 May, the Sultan sent a Kelantan ministerial delegation comprising Dato Menteri (the State Secretary) and Dato Bentara Setia (the Sultan's secretary) to Singapore, with a letter reporting the latest situation to the Governor.[12] The timing of the meeting with the Governor, which took place on 18 May, is significant. It occurred three days after the British troops had returned to Singapore, and one day after W.G. Maxwell left Singapore to investigate the causes of the rising. Had the conflict between the Sultan and the British Adviser become so acute that the Sultan feared that the latter had misreported him to the Governor? The three-hour meeting the two ministers had with the Governor was clearly meant to give the Sultan's version of developments in Kelantan. The Governor's report of the interview shows the Sultan as anxious to denounce the rebels and to demonstrate his support for the British force sent to Kelantan.[13]

The report has three parts: (a) a summary of what was said by the two ministers, (b) information given by the ministers in reply to questions put to them by the Governor, and (c) the Sultan's charge that the Pasir Putih district officer, Abdul Latif, was to blame for the rebellion. The Malay ministers tried to convey the impression that from the very beginning of the outbreak the Sultan had taken control of affairs. On 30 April, he had reportedly learned of the disturbance from three sources, one of them being the British Adviser. The Sultan had then ordered both the ministers to accompany the Dato Panglima Prang to Pasir Putih, arrest To' Janggut, and settle the matter. However, they returned to Kota Bahru the same day after meeting the British Adviser at Pringgat, nine miles from Kota Bahru, and learned that the rebels numbered only about 200 and that the matter was being dealt with by the police under Chief Inspector Jackson.

The next day (1 May) assistance was sought by the British Adviser, who told the Sultan that Jackson placed the number of rioters at 2,000 and needed assistance from the Malay chiefs. The latter were to meet with the police force at Bukit Jawa, but instead went ahead to meet with the rebels in Pasir Putih. On 3 May they received a message from Ungku Besar, the rebel leader, seeking a free pardon for all in return for ending the disturbance. However, the Sultan said this was impossible, and the Adviser agreed. On 5 May British troops arrived from Singapore, and the Sultan ordered the chiefs to accompany them. The Governor's report, relaying the chiefs' account, continues:

> On the morning of the 6th May the force marched to Gunong, the Adviser and Dato Setia accompanying them. On arrival at Gunong,

at about 2 p.m., they were informed that the rebels, some 2,000 to
3,000 in number, were stationed at six different places. The force
stayed at Gunong that night.

On the 7th May the Dato Setia saw various loyal natives and
informed them that it was the Sultan's order that they were to help:
in this way some 150 were collected and spoken to by the Adviser.
They also heard that it was the intention of the rebels that half of
them should march against Kota Bahru, the remainder to defend
Pasir Puteh....[14]

The statement that the rebels "were stationed at six different
places" tallies with the information in Col. Brownlow's report, except
that the latter had noted down the locations and the reported rebel
strengths. However, as noted earlier, Farrer and the British Adviser
said this information was "concocted" to delay the arrival of the British
force. Fortunately for the Sultan, the Malay emissaries had met the
Governor at least two weeks before Farrer's report reached him, so that
his suspicions on the Sultan's role had already been allayed and Farrer's
argument was less damaging than it might have been.

Since this interview gave the Sultan's view of events, we need
to consider further what the Malay emissaries said to the Governor.
Much of what was said anticipated the later allegations that Farrer,
Langham-Carter and W.G. Maxell would raise about the Sultan, his
"entourage", and members of the Kelantan royal family, identified as "the
Tungkus" who were accused of involvement in plotting the rebellion.
Under most circumstances, the combined influence and opinion of these
three British officials would have been sufficient to raise doubts in the
Governor's mind about the Sultan's support and loyalty. That this did
not happen was largely due to the preemptive interview the emissaries
had with the Governor.

The Sultan's emissaries provided the Governor with a lengthy
explanation of the origins of the rebellion based on information gathered
from the villagers, who, they said, were angry about taxes. According to
the Sultan's representatives, the villagers were not unwilling to pay taxes,
but were frequently abused by the D.O., Abdul Latif, and his revenue
collectors. The D.O. had not explained that the land rent was in lieu
of the various produce taxes, and if the point had been made clear to
them, they would willingly have paid. The Sultan had received several

petitions against the D.O., and had dealt with them in consultation with the Adviser; none had come before the State Council. The rebel leader To' Janggut did not refuse to pay the tax, they said, but claimed he had no money. The police sergeant was killed while trying to handcuff the old man.

The Governor questioned the emissaries closely after hearing their version of the events of the rebellion.[15] The emissaries' answers reconfirmed that the Sultan was loyal to the British, happy that the British force had been sent to Kelantan, did not see the rebellion as an anti-British action and disavowed any connection whatsoever with the rebels. The Governor summarised some of these statements in his report to the Colonial Office:

— They had not heard the rising was directed against white people. It had nothing to do with Turkey being at war with England.
— The Sultan was afraid of the rioters and was very glad to see the English soldiers. The Dato Setia states that he thinks that there would have been trouble if the soldiers had not arrived.
— To restore quiet the five leaders of the rebellion should be captured and even if they are not captured and the villagers find that the Government will not deal harshly with them matters will become quiet. It is desirable, however, that some of the Indian soldiers should be left at Kelantan for a time.
— Ungku Besar, the leader of the rebellion at Pasir Puteh, was grandson of Ungku Seliah who was a friend of the Sultan and held a high position at Pasir Puteh. Ungku Besar is unknown [sic] to the present Sultan, but the reasons which led him to raise the rebellion are unknown.[16]

The Governor's comments show that he was convinced that the Sultan was clearly on the side of the British authorities, and therefore in need of the Governor's full support. This support, as it transpired later, was crucial in determining the outcome of the conflict between the Sultan and the British Adviser, and led to the latter's ouster. In summing up the Governor submitted the following views to the Colonial Secretary:

I have written at some length as to what took place at the interview as I consider it of importance that you should be placed in full knowledge of the information and views given to me by the high officials deputed by His Highness the Sultan to see me on this matter.

I consider that there was no doubt some discontent on the part of the villagers on the land rent, the incidence of which had not been properly explained to them. The Ungku Besar was aware of this discontent and believed that it was a favourable opportunity to fan the grievance and make himself, as his grandfather was, a power at Pasir Puteh. He no doubt came to the wrong conclusion in considering that the Sultan could not on account of the war expect help from Singapore and that his own followers were sufficient to deal with those of the Sultan. The English troops returned to Singapore on the 17th May but in the meantime a detachment of the Malay States Guides would remain at Kelantan to assist the Sultan to maintain order.[17]

As explained above, the Sultan's emissaries were able to neutralize the negative views of British officials that soon arrived on the Governor's desk. This strategy was a far-sighted one, but other strategies should also be noted. The Sultan did not appear recalcitrant all the time. He often alternated between support and opposition. In fact, he rendered assistance and cooperation voluntarily to the British Adviser on several occasions after the outbreak began. Otherwise the Sultan's "recalcitrance" would have led to a crisis in relations between himself and the British authorities in Singapore, something the Sultan wished to avoid. However, when he was cooperative, he was not totally submissive. In fact, he seems ambivalent — sometimes opposing, sometimes criticising, sometimes taking the initiative and sometimes following the advice of the British Adviser (and sometimes going beyond the call of duty in his support). He was a great actor of many parts. This ambivalence was, therefore, another reason why British officials like Langham-Carter and Farrer suspected his motives.

The Sultan's "Tough" Attitude

The Sultan issued draconian instructions and proclamations against the rebels on several occasions, but it is not clear whether this was done on his own initiative or at the urging of the British Adviser. Ibrahim Nik Mahmood, quoting Kelantan state government sources that have since gone missing in the Malaysian National Archives and thus cannot be verified, suggests that on at least a few occasions the Sultan acted on his own initiative. His interpretation apparently rests on the simple rationale that since the proclamations were issued in the name of the Sultan, he must have initiated or drafted them. However, within the British protectorate, as Ibrahim himself was aware, the use of the Sultan's name camouflaged the British Adviser's role. The Sultan's signature did not necessarily mean that he agreed with the latter's policy. Ibrahim cites one instance of a proclamation issued in the face of To' Janggut's defiance. The Sultan had instructed the *To' Kweng* (village heads) of Bachok, Peringat, Semerak and Gaal — the four Kweng in the area of Pasir Putih to round up the rebels.[18] They were to wear red armbands to distinguish themselves from the rebels. On 13 May, Ibrahim states, the Sultan further "communicated to the British authorities" his intention to place a reward of five hundred dollars for the arrest of each of the rebel leaders, and this was done a week later.[19]

As indicated earlier, it is difficult to verify Ibrahim's observations, as it is not possible to locate and check the Sultan's papers any longer. However, another notice was issued on 23 May, also in the name of the Sultan, requiring each household in Pasir Putih to pay a fine. In this case the file is still available in the Malaysian National Archives, and it indicates that the punitive measure was not the Sultan's idea, but originated from one of the British officials, either Langham-Carter or W.G. Maxwell, both of whom were involved.[20] However, the amount of the fine — ten dollars for a big house, five for a medium one and three for a small one — was determined by the Sultan. The fine was to be paid within fifteen days from the date of service of the Notice, otherwise the house with all its contents would be burned to the ground.

This case presents an interesting example of how the Sultan worked to accommodate the British officials — whether it was the British Adviser's idea or W.G. Maxwell's, it was eagerly seized upon by the Sultan, who then supported and increased the proposed penalty, making it more severe — to demonstrate his support, loyalty and sincerity in denouncing the rebellion in no uncertain terms. Evidence that the idea might have been the British Adviser's or Maxwell's is to be found in Langham-Carter's minute to the Acting Adviser, W. Pryde, requesting him to convene a State Council meeting at the earliest opportunity to discuss the proposal as Langham-Carter had decided to leave for Pasir Putih with W.G. Maxwell to oversee the military action against the rebels:

> I think it will be necessary to adopt some punitive measure for the whole Pasir Putih district, and in this Mr Maxwell concurs. Will you call the Council together at first Opportunity and put to them the advisability of inflicting at once a fine from which no one shall be exempt. Probably a fine of $3 per house all through the District would be the easiest to collect with a penalty of an extra dollar, if not paid within 14 days (say), and a further liability to the destruction of the house after that....[21]

In fact, after reading the minute Maxwell told Langham-Carter that he had mentioned the matter of the fine to the Sultan that morning. According to Maxwell, Langham-Carter minuted to Pryde, "H.H. [His Highness] was in favour of $10.00 per house, etc., but we may leave the figure to the Council. Both H.H. and Mr Maxwell rather incline to $5.00 per house."[22]

The State Council meeting on 22nd May approved the proposal to impose a fine on the Pasir Putih households. The Sultan, who had offered to draft the Notice, had himself suggested penalties higher than the $3 fine initially proposed by Langham-Carter, as Pryde's minute shows:

> H.H. suggested (a) $10 per large house (b) $5 per house of medium size and (c) $3 per small house. I agree. H.H. agreed that every house in the jurisdiction of the D.O. Pasir Puteh should incur such a fine. H.H. suggested that, in the Notice, it should be stated that, if payment was not made in 15 days from the date of the Notice, all the goods in the house should be seized. I demurred. I stated that many people would simply take away their goods and would thus escape scot-free. I stated it to be essential that the houses be burnt, if the fine was not paid. His Highness then agreed. The enclosed notice was drafted by Che Hamid of this office, a modification of the notice drafted in the Balai Besar [Palace].[23]

This fine, Ibrahim Nik Mahmood rightly observed, served as a further provocation to the rebels,[24] and led to their final assault on the Malay States Guides on 24th May, resulting in the death of To' Janggut, the rebel leader.

Scorched Earth and Punitive Measures

Before the fatal shooting of To' Janggut on 24 July, the British authorities had set into motion the biggest manhunt ever seen in the state to try to capture the rebel leaders and their supporters. On 20 May, the Sultan had issued a proclamation offering rewards of $500 each for the capture of five rebel leaders (Ungku Besar, To' Janggut, Penghulu Adam, Haji Said and Cik Sahak), followed a few days later with another list of 20 wanted rebel supporters, 16 of them with a price of $250 on their heads, two (Che Ahmad and Haji Senik) with a bounty of $400 and two more (Pa'ia and Mahmat bin Laboh) with a bounty of $500. Another proclamation was also issued by the Sultan calling on the residents of Pasir Putih to surrender any weapons in their possession. If they failed to do so, and on discovery of weapons in their homes, a fine of $100 would be imposed. Soon after, Penghulu Adam gave himself up and was sentenced to 10 years' jail and fined $1,000. This was followed by the capture of three more rebels, Brahim bin Musa, Pak Mat Seman bin Salam and Penghulu Deraman, from the list of 20. The last two received death sentences, which were later commuted to life imprisonment. Ungku Besar and four others, including Pa'ia, were reported to have fled to the southern Thai province of Bangnara. Langham-Carter wrote a letter to the Thai Deputy Commissioner of the province asking him to arrest the men and detain them until a party was sent over to bring them back to Kelantan. The houses of the rebels in Pasir Putih were all burnt down. The hunt for the rebels extended right to the end of 1915. On 26 October Pa'ia was reported killed, and five Pasir Putih men who took part in locating and killing him claimed the reward.[25]

Considering that the Sultan was sympathetic to the rebels' cause, and opposed to the British military action against the rebels, why did he agree to the imposition of such severe punishments on the rebels? Did he believe that the rebels would regard the fines as British-imposed and therefore vent their wrath on the British? Such a conclusion would be possible only if he believed that the people of Kelantan knew that the British were the real controlling authority in the state, and that his own powers were limited. Unfortunately, there is no way of knowing his thoughts.

British Officials Disagree on the Sultan's Role

However, as Langham-Carter would claim, the Sultan's dissimulation, compromise, accommodation and opposition may well have been part of a political game with the British officials. Certainly, his eventual triumph was due to his correct reading of the minds of his British antagonists. In sending his Malay emissaries to meet the Governor on 17 May, the Sultan cleverly anticipated that the British Adviser would try to influence other British officials and the Governor against him. In their respective individual reports Messrs. Farrer, Maxwell and Langham-Carter did, in fact, submit negative views on the Sultan.

Maxwell's confidential report of 2 June 1915 conveys the views of Langham-Carter about the Sultan's "unwonted opposition" towards the latter, and the difficulties Langham-Carter had encountered with the ruler. However, he exonerated the Sultan from being behind the rebellion. A more serious charge against the ruler is that he displayed "an insolent and truculent attitude" towards Europeans and expressed a belief in the imminent downfall of the British Empire, an attitude he shared with his Kelantanese subjects following the outbreak of the mutiny in Singapore in February 1915.[26] Maxwell noted that this marked change in the Sultan's behaviour only occurred "within the last two months", which included the month of May when the revolt took place. He also said that the Sultan had informed him that the rebel leader Ungku Besar had the support of "Tungkus" of high rank in Kota Bahru. While he defended the conduct of the Pasir Putih district Officer, Abdul Latif, Maxwell blamed the Kelantan government (effectively Langham-Carter) for failing to explain the change in the land tax system.

> A great mistake was made by the Kelantan Government in not taking more care to explain to the peasantry the nature of the alteration in the taxation. This omission will have to be remedied,

for when a tax affects the peasant's most valuable property, and is, in the majority of cases, the only direct tax that he pays, it is essential he should understand it. It is important, too, that he should realize the benefit of having a title for his land.[27]

Farrer, the political officer who would soon assume the post of Acting British Adviser for Kelantan, also exonerated the Sultan. He, however, expressed reservations about the Sultan's "entourage" and alleged that a palace group he identified as "the Tunkus" was behind the plot to launch the rebellion. In his report of 31 May 1915, extracts of which have been quoted earlier, he dismissed the Malay emissaries' recent representations to the Governor as an attempt to find in Abdul Latif, the D.O. of Pasir Putih, a "scapegoat", and he defended him. "Inche Abdul Latif is not a popular man with the people. He is a foreigner, and I think afraid to use his discretion, and therefore inclined to be hard and fast, but his unpopularity is not enough to account for the outbreak," said Farrer. He also believed that the threatened enforcement of Langham-Carter's new land rules was also responsible for the rising. "I think therefore that there was a general feeling of mild discontent prevalent throughout Kelantan," he said.[28]

Differences over the District Officer

Asked by the Governor to respond to the comments of Maxwell and Farrer, Langham-Carter highlighted his differences with the Sultan over Abdul Latif, the D.O. While accepting many of the criticisms made by Maxwell and Farrer, he felt that it was "Kota Bahru which engineered a disturbance at Pasir Putih".[29] Regarding his differences with the Sultan, he referred to the Sultan's charge that native Kelantanese were not being employed as officials and to the behaviour of the D.O. of Pasir Putih.

Very shortly before this outbreak His Highness wrote to me alleging this, but a hurried calculation disclosed that (excluding the Police who of necessity are mostly Kelantanese) the figures were roughly 34 non-Kelantanese to 381 natives of Kelantan....

Officially, the Sultan's major disagreement with Langham-Carter related to the conduct of the D.O. of Pasir Putih. Langham-Carter spoke on the latter's behalf:

Before this, indeed before my arrival (but I had to deal with it) was a series of petitions against Abdul Latif which I am sure originated in the Palace, and which anyway had very strong support there. I went to Pasir Putih on purpose to enquire into them and found them to be largely bogus, tho' the District Officer had been stupid about a road he was making, and lost his temper under very great provocation with a clerk and another man who as far as I remember made patently untruthful allegations about a cattle-pass. In Mr Farrer's presence, His Highness said that this trouble was all Abdul Latif, and that I knew he had lots of petitions against him. After some trouble I got these (4) out of him and they dated back to 1912 or early 1913 and referred as far as one can make out now merely to Abdul Latif enforcing the land rules at the time.

Given the thrust of the above reports, it was clear to the Governor that the conflict between Langham-Carter and the Sultan did not augur well for the British administration, and that Langham-Carter had to share some blame for the Kelantan rising especially over the introduction of the new land rules. Moreover, the reports of Maxwell and Farrer also criticised the way the administration had handled the new land rules.

The Ouster of Langham-Carter

The intensity of the Sultan's feelings toward Langham-Carter can be measured by the fact that he petitioned three times to have him replaced. The first occasion was in March 1915, shortly before the rising, when he learned that Langham-Carter was about to go on leave. He wrote to the Governor asking him to choose one of two British officers whose names he mentioned and who knew Malay well.[30] The Governor promised to consider the matter.[31] The second time was on 4 July when he wrote again to the Governor, saying, "Mr W. Langham-Carter may probably apply for leave and before anyone is appointed to his place" he wished to suggest the name of R.J. Farrer, the political officer.[32] He hoped that his state would become "rich and prosperous in every direction," adding that "such things cannot exist without difficulty unless, however, my friend assists me by sending me an Adviser who has such ambitions as I have, and my country may, I hope, gain a high position and enjoy prosperity." Continuing, the Sultan said, "At present I am of the opinion that Mr R.J. Farrer is an able gentleman who has a thorough knowledge of Malay and Malay customs, and when he has taken up the appointment of Adviser to my Government, it would appear that my wishes had been complied with."[33] The Sultan's insistence that the appointee should have "a thorough knowledge of Malay" may be related to Langham-Carter's inadequate grasp of the language and of Malay customs.[34]

In replying to the Sultan, the Governor said that he had "noted the wish expressed by my friend".[35] The third occasion was in February 1916, when Langham-Carter had begun his leave. In reply to an enquiry by R.J. Farrer, the Acting Adviser, submitted at the request of the Governor, asking whether he wished to have Langham-Carter back as Adviser, the Sultan wrote:

> When I heard this, dire dismay seized me, for my one fixed certain idea is that Mr. Langham-Carter should never come back here as Adviser. I look on such an idea with utter dislike. In this I am all the more determined because at the present time it may be said that Kelantan daily increases in prosperity and daily progress in a direction which gives comfort and security to the people of the country. This prosperity and progress dates from the time when I commenced to work with Mr. Farrer as my Adviser. For this reason I urge my friend to confirm Mr. Farrer as British Adviser. I want Mr Farrer to stay and stay on permanently.[36]

The Governor decided to respect the wishes of the Sultan, and immediately telegraphed the Colonial Office in London, requesting them to inform Langham-Carter that on his return from leave, he would be re-assigned to another post in the Federated States, or in the Straits Settlements.[37] In offering an explanation, the Governor said:

> ... it was clear to me from the information then given to me by Mr. W.G. Maxwell whom I had sent to Kelantan to enquire and report on the disturbances that the relations between the Sultan and the Adviser had changed. The Sultan, in fact, did not any longer view Mr. Langham-Carter with that friendship which is so essential, especially in a "New" State and with Malays.... By paragraph 6 of my Confidential dispatch of the 20th July 1915 I pointed out that I considered that Mr. Langham-Carter had erred in not instructing the District Officers to visit the villages personally and explain the details of the change in the land tax.[38]

* * *

Suspicions of collusion between the palace and Malay peasant rebels not only arose in connection with the 1915 rising, but also in the Terengganu revolt of 1928. Did one influence the other? The Sultan of Kelantan's success in ousting Langham-Carter would have become known to the Terengganu royalty, and might have inspired the hot-tempered Yang Di Pertuan Muda of Terengganu, Tungku Muhammad, after he had ascended the throne on the old Sultan's death in 1918, to attempt to oust J.L. Humphreys, the first British Adviser in Terengganu, a man he had been forced to accept. The ouster of W. Langham-Carter by the Sultan of Kelantan might have served as a model, but Tungku Muhammad's attempt met with utter failure, and led instead to his own ouster by Humphreys and to his replacement by his brother Tungku Suleiman in 1920.[39] Ex-Sultan Muhammad's involvement in the Terengganu revolt of 1928 has not been studied by scholars. However, a British official in London later made an insightful comparison between the Kelantan (1915) and Terengganu (1928) revolts, and expressed the suspicion that in the 1928 revolt ex-Sultan Muhammad's brother, Sultan Suleiman, might have also played a double game:

> The affair [1928] is also compared to that in Kelantan in 1915.... I am not sure that it [the Kelantan revolt] was any more serious than the Terengganu disturbance last year [1928] although it seems to have been so regarded at the time, possibly because people were rather nervous during the war [the Great War]. The dispute then also was over land and the disturbance ran very much the same course: the peasants gathered together somewhat suddenly, achieved considerable immediate success and frightened away the local Malay officials, but melted away as soon as loyal forces appeared on the scene....
>
> It is, however, very usual for disturbances of this sort to collapse completely on meeting some show of force, as may be seen from the various peasant rebellions in English history....
>
> It is clear that the court party generally dislike the present land policy (see e.g. the 1925 incident) and bearing in mind the similar suggestions that the court secretly supported the Kelantan outbreak, I do not think we can completely abandon the suspicion that the Sultan was trying (however ineffectively) to play a double game.[40]

Earlier, with regard to the 1922 disturbances in Terengganu over the land policy, J.L. Humphreys, the then British Adviser in Terengganu, had observed:

> The close parallel to the beginnings of the Kelantan rising of 1915 has been noted by everyone here... But [Terengganu rebel leader] Haji Drahman's genuine sanctity and high character make him a more dangerous leader than a rustic bravo like To' Janggut.... In this affair, as in the Pasir Putih disturbances, the peasants and their leader have been supported, and exploited by influential persons working for their own ends.[41]

Conclusion

The reading of the rebellion found in the British administration archives shows evidence that the Sultan of Kelantan may well have been playing a "double game", a view that is missing from any of the the folk accounts. The Sultan was sympathetic to the issues raised by the rebels, such as the alleged misconduct of the district officer of Pasir Putih and their fears of the new land rules, as evident from the report, which his Malay emissaries presented to the Governor. The court party comprising the "Tungkus" also did not support the new land rules, so that collusion between them and the rebels can not be ruled out.

The Sultan was hesitant, if not ambivalent in the early stages of the rising. He opposed the arrival of the British troops in Pasir Putih, and when this effort collapsed he quickly distanced himself from it and began to support and institute drastic measures to suppress the rebels. As Langham-Carter had observed, "so long as he could do so under cover he has been not less than sympathetic with the real rebels whom he now denounces vaguely and with their objects as far as they were disclosed to him".

Although the Sultan repeatedly blamed the district officer for the rebellion, none of the British officials concurred with this view. Unfortunately for Langham-Carter, Maxwell and Farrer also criticised his policies, and when the Sultan asked that he be replaced by Farrer, the Governor decided that he had to go. Thus, Langham-Carter became another casualty of the rising.

Chapter 11

Conclusion

My intention in this study has been to examine alternative versions of the popular legend of To' Janggut. The 1915 rising in Kelantan is a much-studied topic in Malaysian history. It appeared to me that it would be challenging to deconstruct the folk story of the movement by contrasting this version with its rivals. In bringing together the folk legend and newly available documents from the colonial administration, I hoped to provide a new, composite picture of To' Janggut's romance.

Yahya Abdullah's *Peperangan To' Janggut, atau Balasan Derhaka* (To' Janggut's War, or the Retribution for Rebellion) is often seen as a romanticised folk version of To' Janggut's life. It comprises elements of magic, fantasy and the supernatural, especially in its presentation of his invulnerability cult, charisma, defiance of authority, and propensity to violence and also his disguised pursuit of revenge for his father's death, allegedly following his father's seduction and rape of Wan Serang Bulan, his lord's concubine.

One reason for the lasting appeal of this story is that it can be read as an adventure yarn, a fairy tale (the beautiful concubine seduced, and the dire consequences that follow), or as a morality tale in which those who step outside of acknowledged norms suffer. At another level, it may be read as an attack on the values of Malay feudal society, or on British colonial rule.

To' Janggut's folk image is that of a fighter for freedom, however vague this concept may be, and his defiance of the Sultan's authority has made him unpopular in some circles in Kelantan, but something of a hero in others. Several local Kelantanese accounts omit any mention of the events relating to his father's acts of *lese-majeste*, while other accounts daringly repeat the stories. Furthermore, when asked to lay down his arms and surrender by the Sultan, he refused to do so and was branded a rebel. Consequently, as a punishment for his defiance against the Sultan's authority, on his death his corpse was put on public display, hanging upside down. Children's stories about To' Janggut portray him as an exemplary figure, a good-hearted and religious person, while the folk legend depicts him as a bad-tempered gambler and murderer, but for all that the hero of a romantic adventure story.

The alternative versions of To' Janggut's story are often mutually contradictory, and are at odds with the folk legend, some circumstantially, others directly so. In some official accounts To' Janggut remains a shadowy figure within a mosaic of people's images of what he should be. He is a desperado and leader of thieves. He is a front man, and possibly a dupe. He is related to the Sultan, yet is said to oppose the Sultan and branded a rebel. Among the European officials, only Pepys had some positive things to say of him: "a man of some learning and consequent repute in an unlettered community", apparently referring to his years of study and sojourn in Mecca.

The hanging of his corpse was meant to serve as a lesson for rebelliousness and to end his invulnerability cult, yet contrary to expectations, it was such a shocking spectacle that it evoked great sympathy and support for him among the populace, and turned him into a hero. Later, the administration banned photographic images of him for fear they would encourage sedition and unrest. Unaware of his true appearance, a later generation of Muslim Malay historians and artists depicted him as an Islamic militant who launched a *jihad*, although there is no historical evidence to indicate that his movement invoked political Islam.

If it had not been for To' Janggut's rebellion, it is unlikely that W. Langham-Carter would have been ousted as British Adviser, but he was out-manoeuvred in the politics of the Kelantan palace involving the "Tungkus". The Governor supported the Sultan's conduct during the rebellion, and probably suppressed evidence from the British Adviser about the ruler's kinship ties with To' Janggut and the "double game" he played in the affair.

The To' Janggut rebellion was an example of Malay resistance during the early years of colonial rule. It shows how the palace and the land-owning class could combine with the peasants and initiate a peasant rebellion to oppose British-imposed land reforms. This picture, however, was concealed from public view, and is revealed only in the confidential reports of the British administration. The pattern was repeated later in Terengganu in the disturbances of 1922, 1925 and 1928 in which the palace, the land-owing aristocrats and the peasants combined to oppose land reforms, although its early forms had emerged in the Perak and Pahang rebellions of 1875 and 1895 respectively.

I have tried to tease out of the official records and the other sources a more inclusive story that takes into account To' Janggut's role, but this in no way privileges one version over the others. I have tried through photography to explore the visualisation of To' Janggut by looking at the relationship between texts and visual records, and between photographs and memory. But, even here, in the imaging of To' Janggut, it is difficult to distinguish between memory and history, visual materials and history, and between fiction and reality.

I have called the To' Janggut story a romance. The word "romance" conveys a sense of fantasy, magic and adventure, with an emphasis on the personal, while the word "romantic" emphasises ideals or fantasies at the expense of reality. The anthropologist James Boon offers the following description of "romance", which seems appropriate to the legend of To' Janggut:

> Romance portrays vulnerable, disguised protagonists, partial social misfits who sense surpassing ideals and must prove the ultimate feasibility of actualising those ideals often against magical odds.... Romance properly concerns champions rather than heroes ... they are surrounded by signs and tokens of semi-miraculous birth, prone to mystical insights, and are acquainted with the natural and rustic orders more intimately than their privileged aristocratic counterparts.[1]

To' Janggut's story remains incomplete. Much is still a mystery, much still speculative. Because the folk legend imparts images of heroism and patriotism, he has achieved lasting fame and celebrity. As James Boon suggests, it is around such "vulnerable, disguised protagonists and partial social misfits" that the legends of romantic figures are made.

Appendix

Outbreak in Kelantan: Report of Interviews with People of Pasir Putih, 20 July 1915

(taken from C.O. 273/427/38566, pp. 270–97)

The Interviews

Below are the extracts of statements given by the interviewees:

"A" Statement of Ungku Sahid, peon in the District Office (recorded by W. Langham-Carter, hereinafter abbreviated to W.L.C. on 12 May 1915):

> "I heard nothing of any intention of any row before 29th April 1915 [i.e. the first day of the outbreak]. I don't know about grants, but I heard people say grant fees were dear, and that they had been told by men of Gunong, Pasir Tumboh, etc. I don't know if the District Officer had issued notices to pay the new taxes."[1]

"B" Statement of Pa'Chu Hing, a trader of Pasir Putih (taken down by CPO Jackson on 13 May 1915):

> "I heard the rebels say they were going to wait for the Police from Kota Bharu. They said they wanted to kill the white men, the Sikhs, and the other non-Kelantanese who had imposed heavy taxes since they came. I heard them say they wanted to kill the D.O. [District Officer] and his clerks for stopping the people from selling their goods in the village."
>
> An official commentary on this statement reads: "They were ordered to sell in the market and not in the streets which they made filthy, but no fee was charged. It was a mere conservancy order."

"C" Statement of P[olice].C[onstable?]. Awang, (recorded by Jackson?)

> "To' Janggut complained about heavy taxes this year. He also said
> the District Officer was very hard on the people. If the soldiers
> dare not come, they would pay no taxes and the country would be
> governed by Ungku Besar.[2]

"D" Statement of Usof b. Mohamed, a trader of Pasir Putih (recorded
by Jackson on 7 June 1915):

> "I heard the rebels say if Che Ibrahim, the District Officer's clerk,
> were here, they would split him up and that's how he would pay
> taxes."

"E" Statement of Brahim Batak (date of interview and interviewer's
name not recorded)

> "They complained of the taxes and the number of prosecutions. It
> was said Ungku Besar wished to be Raja. We were told to collect
> in numbers to resist the Police, who were coming to punish us for
> the murder of the Sergeant."[3]

"F" Statement of Imam Kadir, a religious official (recorded by CPO
Jackson on 30 May 1915):

> "The rebels said they did not like the non-Kelantanese to govern
> Pasir Putih."

"G" Statement of Doraman bin Dia (recorded by District Officer of
Pasir Putih Pepys on 25 May 1915):

> "To' Janggut said, 'Let us kill the white men and the Sikhs. It is
> hard for the people while they are here'."

"H" Statement of Penghulu Adam, one of the major leaders of the
rising (recorded by Pepys on 16 May 1915 after he surrendered himself
to the authorities):

> "I don't know why the Sergeant was murdered nor the cause of
> the disturbance. I had heard of dissatisfaction of the people over
> land rents, the new ones. I heard nothing of Ungku Besar wanting
> to relieve the oppression of the people. I have heard of no anger
> against the District Officer personally. I heard the crowd come to
> the Police Station, 'We'll kill the Government servants.' I myself
> was dissatisfied with the new taxes. My land had not been surveyed,

so I was not liable and had no personal feelings. I have heard of dissatisfaction over the market."

The official comments on this statement read: "This man was a prisoner, and his statement is at direct variance with Nebing Awang's statement [Interviewee 'W' below] which shows that he had a direct and acute personal grievance against the old taxes. Though he has an old '*kuasa*' [letter of authority] from H.H. [His Highness the Sultan] delivered by the Tungku Besar, he is head of the P.P. [Pasir Putih] cattle thieves, and most of his statement is probably untrue."

"I" Statement of Tuan Muda (recorded by W.L.C. on 12 May 1915):

"I had heard To' Janggut say the District Officer was hard over the padi and other taxes trying to collect them all at one time instead of separately. The District Officer gave time to those who asked for it. All the same they were angry with him because of the taxes. Not a single summons had been issued for 1915 taxes as far as I know. A lot of people got summonses last year, and that for what they owed last year. I do not think the D.O. was hard. He would always listen to reason. I think the taxes were being collected a little quicker this year than last. I had not heard the big men set the *raiats* [the people] in motion."

The official remarks on this statement, made probably by W.L.C. himself read: "This man seems entirely loyal, gave the D.O. information of the rebels' purpose on the night of 28 April [the eve of the rising] and has helped the Government ever since. H.H. and someone else (I forget who) have made exactly opposite complaints, namely that the D.O. collects the various taxes at various times, won't wait at his collecting stations, and so gives the people the trouble of going to office often. A travelled Iman of Kg. [Kampong] Laboh has expressed to me personally his admiration of the land-tax 'because you pay everything in one just as you do in Penang' — Where, as a matter of fact, you probably pay quit rent and two assessments."

"J" Statement of Tuan Muda (recorded by Pepys on 23 May 1915):

"Ungku Besar who informed my man Teh Wan Nik of the intended attack on Pasir Putih at 5 a.m. tomorrow morning (24 May 1915)[4] also told him that Tungku Chik Penambang was ordering the attack and that it was with the approval of all the Tungkus in Kota Bahru except the Sultan and his sons."

"J1" Statement of Abdul Razak, planter of K. Lebir (taken by Farrer; no date):

> "The new taxes have not been collected nor enforced. Moreover, they will not work out heavier than the old ones, and the people will be no worse off. I think the motive is that the heads of the rebellion hoped that in the present state of affairs (in Europe), a disturbance of this nature would result in Ungku Besar becoming Raja, etc."

"K" Statement of Abdul Razak as above (taken by Jackson on 13 May 1915):

> "The people have no fear of punishments inflicted by the Magistrate, take the law into their own hands and do as they like. The sentences are very light and so many cases are dismissed. I think they could not have thought this out for themselves but some one, who I know not, must have put this idea into their heads."

"L(i)" Statement of H. Mahmud, Kabuli trader of Pasir Putih (taken by Farrer mid-May):

> "I heard rumours the people were making secret arrangements not to pay taxes to Government because the new tax was heavier than the old. Before under native rule they were well off, now under British, they were not. I was asked on 24th April to go up country (and join the rebels) because Government had stopped people selling foodstuffs on the roads and only in the market. I am prepared to say that the whole countryside was in the plot, which was to drive out all foreigners and govern the country themselves. The District Officer was said to be the child of Europeans. Ungku Besar was to be Raja, etc."

"L(ii)" Statement of the above (to Jackson? mid-May):

> "They (the rebel leaders named) had combined against Government. They could not stand the heavy taxes. They asked me to join and said I should do so as men of my race had been shot lately in Singapore."

"M" Statement of Tok Kweng [title for Penghulu in Kelantan] Awang Ga'al (to Pepys on 16 May 1915):

> "I have heard people complain that the rents to be collected in 1915 were very high — they were not men from my district but from outside."

"N" Statement of Che Sahid (to Jackson on 19 May 1915):

> "I was advised to run away as To' Janggut said he would murder all foreigners."

"O" Statement of Warder Kundor (to Jackson on 11 May 1915):

> "District Officer told the Sergeant: the rebels want to destroy the Police Station and take away the Treasury money because they are angry at my trying to collect all the taxes at once. I hear that the clerk Che Brahim [refers to interviewee 'S'] orders the Kampong people to go straight to the Market. He abuses them and kicks over their baskets. He also brings them before the District Officer who fines them $5. I hear he and the District Officer abuse the people."

"P(i)" Statement of H. Daud, school master of Pasir Putih (to Jackson on 11 May 1915):

> "After statement about the D.O. collecting taxes hard and an intention to attack the Police Station because the people were in difficulties over the taxes, and as above as regards prohibition of street selling — My boys told me if To' Janggut's people met any non-Kelantanese they were going to murder them because the non-Kelantanese including Europeans want to rule the country — and I, being Selangor born, was afraid" etc.

"P(ii)" Statement of H. Daud (to Pepys on 24 May 1915):

> "At 8.30 p.m. I heard from Semerak men whom I don't know that all the Sikhs and white men have been killed and that Tunku Chik of Penambang is now at Kuala Semerak having arrived last evening."

"Q" Statement of Che Leh Mualaf, shopkeeper of Pasir Putih (to Jackson on 15 May 1915):

> "The rebels on their way to the Police Station shouted that they wanted the District Officer to pay their taxes (to him). Awang Omar asked for my rings saying, "There is no Raja, save I.""

"R" Statement of Awang Lah, peon in the District Office (to W.L.C. on 16 May 1915):

> "I had heard that people who had lost cases before the District Officer were aggrieved. When I gave out notices about the new permits, people did say the new taxes were heavy. I can't remember

who but not H. Sahid nor Penghulu Adam [both rebels] as they
had no notices for permits. The Nebing [not clear whether he
is referring to interviewee 'W' or 'X'] said the rebels were going
to kill all non-Kelantanese, for since outsiders came in, taxes had
increased a lot."

"S" Statement of Che Brahim bin Lakop, Kelantanese clerk in D.O. (W.L.C. on 21 May 1915):

"I had heard the country men resented having to sell in the Market
and not in the street. I had not heard there were any grievances
about taxes or assaults or anything. I do not go outside much but
this year I did go to Jeram and Gong Datoh and we collected less
than usual. The people only said they had no money and nothing
more. At Jeram many did not plant and those that did, did not
get much. The rains were a failure but the Gong Datoh land was
deep. About six months before, people had been ordered to sell in
the market and not on the road side. About two months before, six
or seven people had been summoned for not taking out a licence
to buy and retail. They were either warned or fined 50 cents each,
I can't remember which."

"T" Statement of Nik Mohammad, Kelantanese clerk in D.O. (to W.L.C. 21 May 1915):

"We went off because we heard the country men were after
Government Servants. I had not heard there was to be any rising
but eight days before when calling Che Hamat in to take a permit,
H. Sahid asked what I wanted him for and when I said, 'To pay
taxes,' he replied, 'Don't call him, people have agreed not to pay
taxes.' After the Sergeant's death, I did not believe in the rumours
till Penghulu Lembek told me, 'To' Janggut is going to drive out all
the Government servants and non-Kelantanese.' I do general work,
go out collecting taxes, etc. I did not hear any grievances about
delays in office, abuse, assaults, taxes or anything. No summonses
have been issued for this year's taxes, but they have for last year's.
It was a lot of summonses. I don't think the padi crop was bad
this year, but there is no trade and (padi) prices have fallen as they
have for coconuts. People said it was hard to pay taxes this year,
but they say that every year. I did not hear people had combined
not to pay, or had petitioned for time. When they ask for time,
the D.O. grants it."

"U" Dolah Timun (to Pepys on 7 July 1915):

> "I hear that To' Janggut (on Sunday before the Sergeant's murder) got a letter from the *orang hilir*, (which he explains as) Tungku Chik Penambang, saying that people were to keep back their taxes. It was all taxes that were to be kept back. I asked Tok Kueng Puteh when the letter had come and he said, 'Quite recently.' He said that To' Janggut had gone himself to Kota Bahru and brought it back to Pasir Puteh. If it was known that I had told this secret, I should be killed," etc.
>
> The official note on this statement reads: "This man has himself received a heavy sentence over this affair."

"V" Statement of Abdul Latif, the District Officer of Pasir Putih (to Pepys on 23 May 1915):

> "I have heard both in Kota Bahru and Pasir Puteh that Tungku Chik Penambang is the head of the rebellion wishing to depose H.H. the Sultan and succeed him after getting rid of all Europeans and other *orang luar* (foreigners)."

"W" Statement of Nebing Awang of Nering (to Pepys on 3 June 1915):

> "When I went round alone on the night of 28 April I saw To' Janggut and Penghulu Adam on the road at Nering. I was afraid to stop and talk to them as both were angry with me because earlier in this year I had served a summons on Penghulu Adam to pay padi-tax for 1914. To' Janggut, a life-long friend of his, resented this. I overheard them saying, 'We are going to get all the people together to make an attack on Pasir Puteh town.' I heard them go on, 'because of the summons which was served on Penghulu Adam'. Three days before I had passed To' Janggut's house and heard his voice and that of Penghulu Adam and Che Sahak. I heard them saying, 'We will attack when convenient.' Penghulu Adam was a constant visitor at To' Janggut's, so too was Che Sahak. H. Sahid was a new friend. He had been going there in the month preceding. The above were always plotting. That is what aroused suspicions. Penghulu Adam is a head cattle thief, not doing the stealing himself. He had several agents, such...There was dissatisfaction among the people because they had no money to pay taxes, but they only asked for time to pay. They did not say they would fight Government."

"X" Statement of Nebing Tok Dolah of Jeram (to Pepys on 26 May 1915):

> "Two days after the attack on Pasir Puteh (on 29 April 1915) Ungku Besar came to my house. I asked him what is the cause of this disturbance? He replied that he consulted the Tungku Perkoma Rajah as to the people's difficulties about taxes and the latter said that if the people had no money to pay at present they could hang on (and pay later when they had). I replied, 'That is excellent advice but does not explain the violence.' Ungku Besar replied, 'To' Janggut insists on fighting all the same.'"

"Y" Statement of Che Mat, Chief Clerk in D.O. at Pasir Putih (to Pepys on 26 June 1915):

> "When I was going to Kota Bahru from Pasir Puteh after the first attack, I met near Gunong some men who asked me whether it was true Pasir Puteh was sacked. They said, "This is not the people's doing. It is well known that it was arranged by three Rajas (1) Tungku Chik Penambang (by his Siamese name, Tungku Phra Ahmat) (2) Tungku Petra Dalam Kebun (3) Tungku Sri Mas, or Maharajah."
>
> The official note on this statement reads: "Che Mat added that he did not believe this."

Notes

Chapter 1

1 London: Abacus, 1997, p. 277.
2 W.A. Graham, *Kelantan: A State of the Malaya Peninsula. A Handbook of Information* (Glasgow: James Maclehose and Sons, 1908), p. 41.
3 Cyril Skinner, *The Civil War in Kelantan in 1839* (Singapore: Monograph of the Malaysian Branch of the Royal Asiatic Society, 1966).
4 Graham, *Kelantan*, pp. 47–8. On Sultan Senik's harsh rule, British administrator Hugh Clifford has written, "… I have often heard the present Sultan of Pahang speak with horror of the frequency with which he [Sultan Senik] awarded punishment by death and mutilation to any of his people who were convicted or accused of comparatively small offences. This account of his manner of governing Kelantan is fully corroborated by the older natives of that State who remember him in his prime, and who have often told me tales of his cruelty." See Hugh Clifford, "Report on the Expedition to Trengganu and Kelantan, 1895", *Journal of the Malayan Branch of the Royal Asiatic Society* 36, 1 (May 1961): 107.
5 *Report on the State of Kelantan, for the year August 1903 to August 1904*, (Bangkok, 1904), p. 26. The report was written by Graham as Siamese Adviser.
6 Ibid., p. 3.
7 See Graham's *Report on the State of Kelantan for the year August 1903 to August 1904*, pp. 26–7.
8 James de Vere Allen, "The Kelantan Rising of 1915", p. 250. The "Federated Malay States" (FMS) had been formed in 1896 comprising Negri Sembilan, Selangor, Perak and Pahang, the first four states to come under British protection and be ruled by British Residents.
9 For this account on land tax reforms, I have relied on the article by Mohd. Kamaruzaman A. Rahman, "Penasihat Inggeris: Pembaharuan Pentadbiran

Negeri Kelantan dan Pengukuhan Kuasa (1910–1920)", *Warisan Kelantan* 11 (1992): 56–73.

[10] W.G. Maxwell's confidential report to the Governor, 1 June 1915 in CO 273/427/29921.

[11] Ibid.

[12] See Ibrahim Nik Mahmood, "The To' Janggut Rebellion of 1915", p. 71.

[13] See "Plan of the Kelantan-Besut boundary", Kelantan 218/16, enclosures between 4 and 16 March 1916. The plan was first drafted in 1914.

[14] W.G. Maxwell's confidential report, dealing with the causes of the outbreak, 1 June 1915.

[15] *The Straits Times*, 29 May 1915.

[16] See Yahya Abdullah, *Peperangan Tok Janggut, atau Balasan Derhaka.*

[17] Mohd. Kamaruzaman A. Rahman, "Penasihat Inggeris", p. 70. W.G. Maxwell, Colonial Secretary in Singapore, claims he was the grandson of Tengku Sri Maha, while another British official, R.J. Farrer, says he was the grandson of "Ungku Seliah, who was virtual ruler of Pasir Putih district". For Maxwell's report, 1 June 1915, see CO 273/426/29921, and Farrer's report, dated 31 May 1915, in CO 273/42738566.

[18] In their respective official reports on the causes of the rising, R.G. Farrer and W.G. Maxwell blamed Langham-Carter's administration for not explaining to the people the implications of the new land tax system. See Farrer's report, dated 31 May 1915 in CO 273/427/38566 and W.G. Maxwell's report, dated 1 June 1915, in CO 273/426/29921.

[19] Ibrahim Nik Mahmood, "The To' Janggut Rebellion of 1915", p. 72.

[20] Farrer's report, 31 May 1915, in CO 273/427/38566.

[21] Carveth Wells, *Six Years in the Malay Jungle* (London: William Heinemann, 1927), p. 187.

[22] Ibid.

[23] See W.E. Pepys, "A Malayan Side-Show during World War I", *Asiatic Review* 46 (1950): 1174–9.

[24] Ibid.

[25] See A.G. Morkill's note for Rhodes House Library on the rising in 1915, attached to his Diary on Kelantan, MSS. Indian Ocean. S66, 67, undated.

Chapter 2

[1] There are a number of additional story books about To' Janggut that I have not been able to locate. Among these are *Sejarah Hidup Tok Janggut* (in Jawi) by Abdullah Al-Qari (Kota Bharu: Pustaka Aman Press, 1967); and *Pahlawan Bangsa: Tok Janggut Orang Besar Tanahair* by Darus Ahmad (Penang: Sinaran Brothers, 1958).

2   Ibrahim Nik Mahmud, "The To' Janggut Rebellion of 1915", in *Kelantan: religion, society and politics in a Malay state*, ed. William R. Roff (Kuala Lumpur: Oxford University Press, 1974), pp. 62–86.

3   Abdullah Zakaria bin Ghazali, "Kebangkitan Tok Janggut dalam Konteks Gerakan Anti-British di Malaysia", in Nik Anuar Nik Mahmud, *Tok Janggut: Perjuang atau Penderhaka?* [Tok Janggut: Fighter or Traitor?] (Bangi: Jabatan Sejarah, Universiti Kebangsaan Malaysia, 1999), pp. 43–61.

4   Islas alias Ariffin Ismail, "Peperangan Tok Janggut atau Balasan Derhaka, karya Yahya Abdullah (Y'Abdullah): Satu Penilaian mengenai Perjuangan Tok Janggut", Mini Thesis for 1983/1984, History Department, Universiti Sains Malaysia, Penang, p. 25.

5   James de V. Allen, "The Kelantan Rising of 1915: Some Thoughts on the Concept of Resistance in British Malayan History", *Journal of Southeast Asian History* 9 (Sept. 1968): 253–5.

6   Yahya Abdullah, *Peperangan Tok Janggut, atau Balasan Derhaka* [Jawi] (Kota Bharu: Muslim Printing Press, 1955).

7   The mutiny broke out on Monday, 15 February 1915. For a full-length account of the mutiny, see R.W.E Harper and Harry Miller, *Singapore Mutiny* (Singapore: Oxford University Press, 1984).

8   See the Governor's report to the Colonial Office in London on his meeting with the ministers, dated 18 July 1915, in CO 273/427.

9   See the confidential report by W.G. Maxwell, Colonial Secretary, dealing with the causes of the outbreak and containing suggestions and recommendations, 1 June 1915, CO 273/426/29921.

10 Ibid.

11 See Allen, "The Kelantan Rising of 1915", and Ibrahim Nik Mahmood, "The To' Janggut Rebellion of 1915".

12 Allen, "The Kelantan Rising of 1915", pp. 247, 251.

13 Tan Ban Teik, "The To' Janggut Rebellion of 1915 in Kelantan: A Reinterpretation", in *Tokoh-Tokoh Tempatan* [Local-Level Leaders], ed. Cheah Boon Kheng, Occasional Papers No. 2, School of Humanities (Penang: Universiti Sains Malaysia, 1982), pp. 97–113.

14 Ibrahim Nik Mahood, "The To' Janggut Rebellion of 1915", pp. 64–86.

15 Tan Ban Teik, "The To' Janggut Rebellion of 1915 in Kelantan".

16 See Maxwell's confidential report to the Governor, 2 June 1915, in CO 273/426/29921 and W. Langham-Carter's memorandum to the Governor, 12 July 1915, in CO 273/427/38566.

17 See W.G. Maxwell's confidential report, 1 June 1915, CO273/426/29921.

18 J.M. Gullick, *Rulers and Residents: Influence and Power in the Malay States, 1870–1920* (Singapore: Oxford University Press, 1992), p. 209. For other references in the book to the Kelantan rebellion, see also pp. 191–2.

[19] Lawrence Stone, "History and Post-Modernism", *Past and Present*, 135 (May 1992): 197–8.

[20] J. Appleby, L. Hunt and M. Jacob, *Telling the Truth about History* (New York and London: W.W. Norton, 1995), pp. 246–7, 265.

[21] Cheah Boon Kheng, "The Erosion of Ideological Hegemony and Royal Power and the Rise of Postwar Malay Nationalism, 1945–46", *Journal of Southeast Asian Studies* 19, 1 (March 1988): 1–26.

Chapter 3

[1] See S. Othman Kelantan, "To' Janggut: Sebuah Citra Pahlawan", paper presented at the seminar, "Perjuangan To' Janggut", 27–28 August held in Kota Bharu at Balai Islam Lundang. The seminar was jointly organised by the Persatuan Mahasiswa Kelantan Darul Naim, Perbadanan Muzium Negeri Kelantan and Jabatan Sejarah, Universiti Kebangsaan Malaysia.

[2] This description appears in Abdullah Al-Qari bin Haji Salleh, *Detik-Detik Sejarah Kelantan* (Kota Bharu: Pustaka Aman Press, 1971), p. 115. It is the revised edition of Sa'ad Shukri Haji Muda's *Sejarah Kelantan* [Jawi] (Kota Bharu: Penerbit Kelantan, 1962). According to the scholar Kassim Ahmad, the term *musuh* in the Kelantanese dialect means "war". See Kassim Ahmad, "Sha'ir Musuh Kelantan", MA thesis, University of Malaya, 1961, p. xii. Kassim Ahmad's study, however, is not about the To' Janggut rebellion, but is on the civil war in Kelantan in 1839.

[3] Until 19 January 1993, when the Malaysian Parliament approved amendments to the Constitution withdrawing from the Malay rulers their immunity from criminal prosecution, any wrongdoing by the rulers and their families could not come under public scrutiny. Until then, any criticism of royalty fell within the purview of *lese-majeste* or "an offence against the sovereign power". For an interesting discussion of the parliamentary decision, see H.P. Lee, *Constitutional Conflicts in Contemporary Malaysia* (Kuala Lumpur: Oxford University Press, 1995), esp. chapter 4, "The Battle over Royal Immunities", pp. 86–99.

[4] For an excellent discussion of the differences between the palace literary or written tradition and the oral tradition of the ordinary people, see Mohd. Taib Osman, *Kesusasteraan Melayu Lama* (Kuala Lumpur: Federal Publications, 1974), pp. 8–32. Mohd. Taib says that in Malay folk tales and legends of the ordinary people there are often elements of class conflict, e.g., in the stories of Pak Pandir, Pak Belalang and Si Luncai. Among the well-known legends of the Malays he cites are "Tuan Puteri Sakdung" and "To' Janggut" (Kelantan), "Dayang Bunting" (Pulau Langkawi) and "Panglima Hitam" (kedah)·

[5] See author's preface, in Yahya Abdullah's *Peperangan Tok Janggut, atau Balasan Derhaka* (in Jawi; Kota Bharu: Muslim Printing Press, 1955), p. 2.

6   See "Kelantan Trouble: The Outbreak and How it was Suppressed", *The Straits Times*, 29 May 1915. See also CO 273/426/29843 which contains a note by the Governor, Straits Settlements to the Colonial Office, London, 2 June 1915, identifying W.G. Maxwell as the author of the article.

7   W.E. Pepys, "Kelantan during World War 1", *Malaya in History* 6(1) (1960): 36–9.

8   Carveth Wells, *Six Years in the Malay Jungle*, pp. 177–8.

9   In the revised version of Yahya Abdullah's account, Ungku Besar is described as "Raja Jeram whose name is Ungku Besar Tuan Ahmad ibnu Al-Marhum Ungku Chik Pendek. He was the fifth descendant of the lineage of Long Gak Pering the ruler who opened Kota Jeram." See *Riwayat Hidup To' Janggut*, p. 7.

10   In a 1972 study, student-researcher Nik Anuar Nik Mahmud interviewed old-time residents in Jeram district and discovered that after his death Tengku Seri Maharajah was succeeded by his son, Tengku Chik, who was appointed *Tok Kweng* (district chief) in line with the new administrative changes. On Tengku Chik's death, his son, Tengku or Ungku (short for Tengku) Besar Tun Ahmad, the *Tok Kweng Muda* (assistant district chief), succeeded him. He decided to challenge the change of his father's status from raja to district chief. (See Nik Anuar Nik Mahmud, "Sejarah Jeram dan Kebangkitan Tok Janggut 1915", unpublished B.A. thesis, History Department at University of Malaya, 1972, pp. 10–1.)

11   Ibid., p. 20.

12   The above details are taken from the revised version of Yahya Abdullah's account compiled by Haji Abdullah b. Amirah Seling Kelantan, *Riwayat Hidup To' Janggut dan Peperangan-nya di Kelantan* [Jawi] (Penang: Sinaran Brothers, 1957), pp. 1–4.

13   Ibid., p. 51.

14   Yahya Abdullah, *Peperangan Tok Janggut*, p. 43.

15   Haji Abdullah b. Amirah Seling Kelantan, *Riwayat Hidup To' Janggut*, p. 53.

16   Published by Muslim Printing Press, Kota Bharu.

17   "Apabila anaknya yang bernama Mat Tahir iaitu abang kepada To' Janggut dibunuh oleh budak raja dengan tidak bersalah, dan raja tidak menghiraukan tuntutannya supaya menjalankan keadilan keatas pembunuh anakya itu, maka naiklah kemarahannya terhadap raja itu dengan menunggu sa'at sahaja hendak membuat angkaranya."

18   "Satibanya Haji Hasan ke kampung Jeram didapatilah betul bagaimana perkhabarannya itu. Maka naiklah dendam di hatinya hendak menuntut bela di atas kematian bapanya itu."

19   Ariffin bin Abdul Rashid, *Peristiwa-peristiwa di Kelantan* (Kota Bharu: Muslim Printing Press, 1960), p. 51.

[20]   See Sa'ad Shukri, *Sejarah Kelantan* [Jawi], p. 101. I am grateful to Dr Fatimah Busu for making available her personal copy.

[21]   See Sa'ad Shukri bin Haji Muda and Abdullah Al-Qari, *Detik-Detik Sejarah Kelantan* (Kota Bharu: Penerbit Kelantan, 1971), pp. 115–21.

[22]   See Mohd. Hashim Khalin bin Haji Awang, *Dari zaman ke zaman*, pp. 115–9.

[23]   Ibrahim Nik Mahmood, "The To' Janggut Rebellion of 1915", in *Kelantan: Religion, Society and Politics in a Malay State*, ed. W. R. Roff (Kuala Lumpur: Oxford University Press, 1974), pp. 62–86, and Nik Anuar Nik Mahmud, "Sejarah Jeram dan Kebangkitan Tok Janggut (1915)".

[24]   Islas alias Ariffin bin Ismail, "Peperangan Tok Janggut, atau Balasan Derhaka".

[25]   See Gesick, *In the Land of Lady White Blood: Southern Thailand and the Meaning of History* (Ithaca: Cornell University, Southeast Asia Program, 1995), p. 2 and also on p. 70 where the author states, "Every place is both unique and yet part of a larger world, so it is only to be expected and no one is surprised that each place should have a unique story that yet resonates with other stories. A corollary is that there can be no 'definitive version' of any story."

[26]   Tan Ban Teik, "The Tok Janggut Rebellion of 1915 in Kelantan", pp. 97–113.

[27]   By Teks Publishing, Kuala Lumpur.

[28]   See S. Othman Kelantan, "To' Janggut: Sebuah Citra Pahlawan", Paper presented at "Seminar dan Pameran Perjuangan To' Janggut", 27–28 Aug. 1996, p. 7. This seminar, held at Balai Islam Lundang, Kota Bharu, was jointly organised by the Persatuan Mahasiswa Kelantan Darut Naim, Perbadanan Muzium Negeri Kelantan and Jabatan Sejarah, Universiti Kebangsaan Malaysia.

[29]   Ibid., pp. 4–5.

[30]   Ibid., p. 10.

[31]   Ibid., p. 14.

[32]   W.E. Pepys, "A Malayan Side-Show During World War 1", p. 1179.

Chapter 4

[1]   See Islas alias Ariffin Ismail, "Peperangan Tok Janggut, atau Balasan Derhaka", pp. 1–3.

[2]   The translation is based on the romanised transliteration done by my former undergraduate student, Islas alias Ariffin Ismail in ibid., pp. 31–62.

[3]   It was the "fourth district" in terms of listing. Siam's Adviser W.A. Graham had divided Kelantan into five districts and the list was as follows: Kota Bharu, Batu Mengkebang (later renamed as Ulu Kelantan), Kuala Kelantan, Pasir Putih and Kuala Lebir. Only the first two and Pasir Putih districts came into existence.

4 According to one source, the first District Officer of Pasir Putih was one, Encik Ibrahim, who resigned and was succeeded in 1911 by Encik Leh, head of the High Court. See Ibrahim Nik Mahmud, "The To' Janggut Rebellion of 1915", p. 71.

5 The British Adviser's post at that moment was held by W. Langham-Carter.

6 This is certainly an exaggeration. The number did not exceed 100–150 men.

Chapter 5

1 The information about *Truth* was disclosed by W.E. Pepys in his article, "A Malayan Side-show during World War I", p. 1178.

2 *Kelantan Administration Report for 1915* by R.J. Farrer, Acting British Adviser (Kuala Lumpur, Government Printing Office, 1916), p. 13.

Chapter 6

1 The interviews took place between 5 May and 7 July 1915. The people represented a cross-section of the local population, from those in the upper strata such as the Malay aristocracy, with the title of Tungku, down to planters, a village headman, office peons, policemen, captured rebels, Chinese shopkeepers and Indian Muslim traders.

2 This is to be found in the file CO 273/427, pp. 270–97, entitled "Kelantan Re: outbreak in", in despatch by High Commisioner Sir Arthur Young to Secretary of State for the Colonies, A. Bonar Law, 25 July 1915.

3 See "J" Statement of Tun Muda recorded by Pepys on 23rd May 1915, in C.O. l273/427/38566, p. 279.

4 Memorandum by W. Langham-Carter on Maxwell's Confidential, 12 July 1915 in HC des. 167/1915; see also CO 273/427/38566, p. 262.

5 Ibid., pp. 7 and 8 of Langham-Carter's Memorandum.

6 All extracts are from C.O.273/427/38566, 25 July 1915, pp. 270–97. For the full report, see Appendix.

Chapter 7

1 See Memorandum by W. Langham-Carter to Governor, 12 July 1915 in HC Des 167/1915, National Archives of Singapore.

2 See Carveth Wells, *Six Years in the Malay Jungle* (William Heinemann, 1927), pp. 177–8.

3 The 15-page memorandum is found in Colonial Office file CO 273/427/38566.

4 See Langham-Carter's memorandum to the Governor, 12 July 1915, HC Des. 167/1915, National Archives, Singapore, p. 9.

5 This was an appointment agreed to by both the British government and the Trengganu Sultan, who had refused to bring his state under British protection, an event which did not occur until 1919. Despite this status,

however, the British Consul was able to exert some influence on the administration of the state's affairs.

6   See Langham-Carter's memorandum to the Governor, 12 July 1915, HC Des. 167/1915, National Archives, Singapore, pp. 9–10.

7   See Farrer's report, dated 31 May 1915, in CO 273/427/38566.

8   W.G. Maxwell's confidential report, 1 June 1915, in CO 273/427/38566.

9   W. Langham-Carter's confidential memorandum, 12 July 1915, in CO 273/42738566.

Chapter 8

1   Roland Barthes, *Camera Lucida* (London: Vintage, 1993), pp. 5–6.

2   Ibid., p. 14.

3   See his recollections, W.E. Pepys, "A Malayan Side-show during World War", p. 1178.

4   Ibid.

5   Pepys, "A Malayan Side-show during World I", pp. 1174–9. With regard to Pepys reference to To' Janggut's Arab extraction, Allen, mentions that a brief and what he describes as a "typically deprecating account of the Kelantan rising by a former British administrator, emphasising its triviality and suggesting that its leader, To' Janggut, may have had Indian blood (because he had a beard)", appears in *Malaysia*, the British Association of Malaysia's magazine of April 1968. See Allen, "The Kelantan Rising of 1915", p. 241fn.

6   Susan Sontag, "The Image-Builder from *On Photography*", in *A Susan Sontag Reader*, Introduction by Elizabeth Hardwick (Harmondsworth, England: Penguin Books, 1982), p. 359.

7   At the time, she was on sabbatical leave prior to her retirement in 2001 from her position as a lecturer in history with the School of Humanities, Universiti Sains Malaysia in Penang.

8   Tan Liok Ee's e-mail to me, dated 5 December 1998.

9   Tan Liok Ee's e-mail to me, dated 7 December 1998.

10   Roland Barthes, *Camera Lucida*, p. 79.

11   Richard J. Evans, *In Defence of History* (London: Granta Books, 1997), p. 230.

Chapter 9

1   Taken from Stanzas 222, 225 and 276 of Trengganu court poet Tungku Dalam Kalthum's long poem *Riwayat Terengganu Daruliman*. Tungku Dalam Kalthum accompanied her father, Sultan Zainal Abidin III of Terengganu to Kelantan on an official visit a few days after the outbreak of the rebellion. In her long poem *Riwayat Terengganu Daruliman (R.T.D.*

for short), she devotes more than 30 stanzas to the outbreak. The *R.T.D.* was published in Singapore in 1936. The stanzas, translated above, are taken from the poem transliterated into Rumi by Professor Muhammad Yusoff Hashim, in his detailed study, *Terengganu Darul Iman: Tradisi Persejarahan Malaysia* (Kuala Lumpur: Dewan Bahasa dan Pustaka, 1991), p. 553. The aristocrat referred to by Tengku Dalam Kalthum is better known as "Engku Besar" or "Ungku Besar" of Nerang.

2 Farrer's report to the Governor, 31 May 1915, in CO 273/427/38566.

3 Morkill's diary, 2 Oct. 1915, Rhodes House Memorial Library, Oxford.

4 See confidential report by W.G. Maxwell dealing with the causes of the outbreak and containing suggestions and recommendations, in CO 273/426/29921, pp.427–8. A Colonial Office official in London, in a minute on Maxwell's report dated 9 July 1915, commented on two of the "Tungkus" he mentioned as follows: "Tungku Besar and Ungku Chik are two of the 'wicked uncles' [of the Sultan], men of low intellect and vicious character who gave much trouble to the Siamese Adviser [W.A. Graham] before Kelantan was taken over [by the British] in 1909." See the minute in CO 273/435/30576.

5 CO 273/427. Cited in previous chapter, see also the statement of interviewee "V", Abdul Latif.

6 Memorandum by W. Langham-Carter on Maxwell's confidential report of 92/15 to Governor, 12 July 1915 in HC Des 167/1915, National Archives of Singapore; see also the incomplete copy sent to London in CO 273/427/38566, pp. 264–5.

7 See the statements of the interviews in the previous chapter.

8 Ibid., the statement of Che Mat, as told to Pepys on 26 May 1915, cited as interviewee "Y" in previous chapter.

9 See copy of Notice in Jawi, issued by the Kelantan Government (Kel. 531/15), with English translation, in file Kel. PB562/1915, 21 May 1915, and also in British Adviser's file, Kel.PB 552/1915 "Proclamations of rewards for capture, etc. of leaders of rebels", 18 May to 10 June 1915.

10 W. Langham-Carter's Memorandum to the Governor, 12 July 1915, HCD 167/1915, p. 11.

11 Ibid., p. 10.

12 Governor Arthur Young to Colonial Office, 18 May 1915, CO 273/426/28715, p. 6.

13 See the version published in *The Straits Times*, 29 May 1915. The anonymous author was, in fact, W.G. Maxwell, who was sent by the Governor to investigate the rising.

14 Ibid.

15 In a letter which he despatched to the Colonial Office in London, dated 12 May 1915, the Governor wrote: "There was some difficulty regarding

the collection of land-rent, which had been imposed in lieu of the produce-tax; and on 29 April the Assistant District Officer, a Malay, sent the police sergeant, a Kelantan Malay, to make enquiries. The people apparently refused to pay the land-rent, and the sergeant told them that they must go with him to the court. They objected, and he arrested and hand-cuffed an elderly Malay, by whose son he was then stabbed." See HC Des. 125/1915, National Archives, Singapore. Subsequently, Langham-Carter, R.J. Farrer and W.G. Maxwell in their reports made it clear that it was not "the Assistant District Officer" who was involved, but the "District Officer", and that it was To' Janggut who first stabbed the police sergeant and not "his son". In the preamble of his 12th May letter, the Governor had lamented as follows: "I am still without any report upon the subject from the British Adviser. From an unofficial source I have received the following account and have no reason to believe that it is not substantially correct." This delay may have turned the Governor against Langham-Carter later.

[16] R.J. Farrer's report to Governor, 31 May 1915, CO 273/427/38566, p. 5.

[17] Farrer's confidential report to the Governor, 31 May 1915, op. cit.

[18] See *The Straits Times,* 29 May 1915.

[19] See Langham-Carter's memorandum to the Governor, 12 July 1915 in HC Des 167/1915, National Archives of Singapore.

[20] Ibid.

[21] See the evidence given by Awang bin Awang in the case of Awang Hat bin Mat Tahir, who was sentenced to $400 fine or two years' imprisonment on a charge of rebellion, in the magistrate's court (Pasir Putih). See magistrate's file in M200/1915 for rebellion, petition filed by his brother for the papers, 1 Dec. 1915.

[22] See the evidence of Awang Hamat bin Seludin in the case of Awang Hat bin Mat Tahir, ibid.

[23] See the evidence of Brahim bin Botok in the case of Penghulu Lembek, who was convicted and sentenced to one year's imprisonment and a fine of $350 on 18 June 1915 for rebellion. The prisoner filed an appeal against the sentence. See his appeal and trial papers in Magistrate's Court (Pasir Putih) file, Kel. 15/1915.

[24] See R.J. Farrer's report to Governor, 31 May 1915, CO 273/427/38566, p. 4.

[25] See the case of Haji Ngah bin Mahat, file Makhamah Pasir Putih 129A/1915, p. 9.

Chapter 10

[1] See Gullick, *Rulers and Residents.*

[2] Pepys, "Kelantan during World I", p. 37. Robert Heussler also mentions this reprimand in his book *British Rule in Malaya: The Malayan Civil*

Service and Its Predecessors, 1867–1942 (Westport, Connecticut: Greenwood Press, 1981), p. 207.

3   See Governor to the Secretary of State for the Colonies, 5 May 1915, in CO 273/426/26344.

4   Report of R.J. Farrer, 31 May 1915, to Colonial Secreary, Straits Settlements, in CO 273/427/38566.

5   Heussler, *British Rule in Malaya*, p. 207.

6   See the lengthy article, "Kelantan Trouble. The Outbreak and how it was suppressed. Rebel leader killed", *The Straits Times*, 29 May 1915, copy in HCO 1225/1915, Arkib Negara Malaysia. Another copy of *The Straits Times* article, together with the Governor's note, identifying W.G. Maxwell as the author of the article, is found in CO 273/426/29843. For a copy published by *The Singapore Free Press*, 29 May 1915, see the enclosure attached to W.G. Maxwell's type-written confidential report to the Governor in CO 273/426/29921. The Governor's note to the Colonial Office, dated 2 June 1915 in CO 273/426/29843 reads: "I have the honour to forward a copy of an official narrative of the recent outbreak in Kelantan. It was prepared with a view to publication in the local newspapers by Mr. W. George Maxwell, Acting Secretary to the High Commissioner, whom I sent to Kelantan for the purpose of making an independent inquiry and, with the consent of the General Officer Commanding, it was published by the local papers a few days ago."

7   Farrer's report, 31 May 1915, in CO 273/427/38566.

8   *The Straits Times*, 29 May 1915; see also *The Singapore Free Press*, 29 May 1915.

9   Farrer's report in CO 273/427/38566.

10 See report of Lt. Col. C.W. Brownlow, Commander, Kelantan Field Force, 16 May 1915, to Headquarters, Straits Settlements, in CO 273/426/29141.

11 See report of Lt. Col. C.W. Brownlow, Commander, Kelantan Field Force, 16 May 1915, to Headquarters, Straits Settlements, in CO 273/426/29141.

12 Ibrahim Nik Mahmood, "The To' Janggut Rebellion of 1915", p. 63, states that the Sultan's mission was sent, after consultation with the Malay members of his State Council and the British Adviser. He does not mention whether the idea came from the Sultan, or the Adviser, but the "defensive" performance of the Malay Ministers during the interview with the Governor suggests that the mission was the Sultan's idea.

13 Governor's report to Colonial Office, 18 May 1915, in CO 273/427.

14 Ibid.

15 Ibid.

16 Ibid.

[17] Ibid.

[18] Ibrahim Nik Mahood, "The To' Janggut Rebellion of 1915", p. 78, cites the Sultan's directive to To' Kweng and Inspector of To'Kweng, encl. in Kel. PB.108/1915. This file is now missing in Arkib Negara Malaysia.

[19] Ibid., p. 80, citing the Sultan's letter to G.L. Ham (at British Adviser's Office), 29 Jamadal-akhir 1333 (13 May 1915), in Kel. PB126/1915. See also the Notice dated 20 May 1915, encl. in Kel.PB552/1915.

[20] See the file Kel. 562/1915. This is the British Adviser's file, not a palace file as cited by Ibrahim.

[21] W. Langham-Carter to A.A. (Acting Adviser), W. Pryde, dated 21 May 1915, in Kel.562/1915.

[22] Ibid.

[23] Minute of W. Pryde, 22 May 1915, in Kel.562/1915.

[24] Ibrahim Nik Mahmood, "The To' Janggut Rebellion of 1915", p. 82.

[25] See the information in file BAK Kel.1137/15 Arkib Negara Malaysia.

[26] Maxwell's confidential report in CO 273/426/29921.

[27] W.G. Maxwell's confidential report, 1 June 1915, in CO 273/427/38566.

[28] Farrer's report in CO 273/427/38566.

[29] See his memorandum, dated 12 July 1915, p. 10, in CO 273/427/38566. See also the complete "unexpurgated" version in HC Des 167/1915 at National Archives, Singapore.

[30] See the Sultan's letter, dated 6 Mar. 1915, in which he wrote: "Mr McArthur in the Singapore Government Service and Mr Scott are well acquainted with the Malay language and if either of these officers takes up the appointment of Adviser in Kelantan, I shall be satisfied with the carrying out of the administration of the state." Kel. 358/1915.

[31] The Governor's reply, 17 Mar. 1915, in ibid.

[32] See the Sultan's letter to the Governor, 4 July 1915, in Kel.780/1915.

[33] Ibid. Robert Heussler provided some personal details about Farrer in his book, *British Rule in Malaya*, p. 208. Farrer joined the administrative service as a cadet in 1896, and arrived in Kelantan as "captain of the volunteers", that is, the Penang Malay Volunteers, that replaced the Shropshire Light Infantry as a garrison force within the state. "An Etonian and Balliol man, Farrer was able, hardworking, and well regarded in Singapore. He eventually received a C.M.G. (Companion of the Order of St. Michael and St. George, an honour bestowed by the British sovereign), and it was said he would have reached the heights but for a certain unconventionality that did not always sit well with his superiors. He married a non-European [a Malay woman]. After retirement in 1931, he came to Kelantan and lived in a Malay house near the beach at Semerak."

[34] See the interesting observations of Mohd. Kamaruzaman A. Rahman in "Penasihat Inggeris", pp. 71–2.

35 Governor to Sultan of Kelantan, 14 July 1915, in Kel.780/1915.

36 The Sultan of Kelantan to Governor, 8 Feb. 1916, in CO 273/444/14836.

37 Governor Sir Arthur Young to Secretary of State for the Colonies, 25 Feb. 1915, in CO 273/444/14836. Young, however, tried to make it a condition that the Sultan should pay the difference between Langham-Carter's Adviser salary and the salary of the post to which he would have to be "promoted" in the Federated States.

38 Ibid. The expression "New State" refers to the fact that Kelantan had only recently come under British protection under the terms of the 1909 Anglo-Siamese treaty.

39 For a fine account of this episode, see Heather Sutherland, "The Taming of the Terengganu elite", in *Southeast Asian Transitions: Approaches through Social History*, ed. Ruth T. McVey (New Haven: Yale University Press, 1978).

40 See Cairn's minute of 8 Jan. 1929 in the file, "Trengganu Disturbances", CO 717/61/52432/1928.

41 See Humphreys' "Report on certain matters connected with one Haji Drahman of Trengganu", 24 Nov. 1922, in CO 273/717/61/1928.

Chapter 11

1 James Boon, *The Anthropological Romance of Bali: Dynamic Perspectives in Marriage and Caste, Politics and Religion* (Cambridge: Cambridge University Press, 1977), p. 3.

Appendix

1 Under the new land tax system, land titles were granted to owners for the first time, for which they had to pay an annual fee. This single tax replaced the produce taxes, which those who worked the lands had to pay in the past.

2 "Ungku Besar" is clearly identified as the patron of To' Janggut and the main ringleader of the Pasir Putih rising. It is stated in the official statements that he bitterly resented having to pay the new land rent tax, as he had previously been exempted from the payment of produce taxes and head tax in the past.

3 Ungku Besar's desire to be an independent ruler or Raja of Pasir Putih is recorded in the Kelantanese folk account recorded by Yahya Abdullah, *Peperangan Tok Janggut, atau Balasan Derhaka.*

4 This was the fateful attack led by To' Janggut in which he was killed by the soldiers of the Malay States Guides.

Bibliography

MANUSCRIPT MATERIAL
Arkib Negara Malaysia [National Archives Malaysia]

Kel. K. Files of the British Adviser's Office and Secretariat, known as the "K" series, 1915. 1909–16
Kel. PB. Files of the "Pejabat Balai Kerajaan", or Palace Office, 1915

MICROFILMS
The Colonial Office Correspondence, C.O. 273 and C.O. 717 series, (1903–16)

PRINTED MATERIALS
Annual Reports for Kelantan, 1903–16

NEWSPAPERS
The Straits Times, April–August 1915
The Straits Echo, April–August 1915
Utusan Melayu, April–November 1915

National Archives Singapore
High Commissioner's Correspondence, 1915
Governor's Correspondence, 1915

Bodleian Library, Oxford
A.G. Morkill, "Diary of a service in Kelantan", MS., Indian Ocean [S66, S67] kept at Rhodes House Library, Oxford.

Books

Abdullah Al-Qari bin Haji Salleh, *Detik-Detik Sejarah Kelantan.* Kota Bahru: Pustaka Aman Press, 1971.

Abdullah b. Amirah Seling Kelantan, Haji, *Riwayat Hidup To' Janggut dan Peperangan-nya di Kelantan.* Penang: Sinaran Brothers, 1957.

Ariffin bin Abdul Rashid, *Peristiwa-peristiwa di Kelanta.* Kota Bahru: Muslim Printing Press, 1960.

Chan Su-ming, "Kelantan and Trengganu, 1900–1939", *Journal of the Malaysian Branch Of the Royal Asiatic Society* (*JMBRAS*) 38, 1: 159–98.

Che Husna Azhari, *Melor in Perspective.* Bangi: Furuda Publishing House, 1993.

Clifford, Hugh Charles, *In Court and Kampung.* Singapore: Graham Brash, 1989.

Clifford, Hugh, *Report on Expedition to Trengganu and Kelantan,* MBRAS monograph, 34, pt. 1 (May 1961).

Goodwin, James, *Akira Kurosawa and Intertextual Cinema.* Baltimore: The Johns Hopkins University Press, Baltimore, 1994.

Gullick, J.M., *Rulers and Residents: Influence and Power in the Malay States, 1870–1920.* Kuala Lumpur: Oxford University Press, 1992.

Graham, W.A., *Kelantan: A State of the Malay Peninsula.* Glasgow: James Maclehose and Sons, 1908.

Haji Muhammad Saleh bin Haji Awang, *Terengganu Dari Bentuk Sejarah Hingga Tahun 1918.* Kuala Lumpur: Utusan Publications, 1978.

Heussler, Robert, *British Rule in Malaya: The Malayan Civil Service and Its Predecessors.* Westport, Connecticut: Greenwood Press, 1981.

Kessler, Clive S., *Islam and Politics in a Malay State: Kelantan, 1838–1969.* Ithaca: Cornell University Press, 1978.

Lindsey, Timothy, *The Romance of K'tut Tantri and Indonesia.* Kuala Lumpur: Oxford University Press, 1997.

Ladurie, Emmanuel Le Roy, *Love, Death and Money in the Pays D'oc.* Harmondsworth: Penguin Books, 1984.

Lee, H.P., *Constitutional Conflicts in Contemporary Malaysia.* Kuala Lumpur: Oxford University Press, 1995.

Mohd. Taib Osman, *Kesusasteraan Melayu Lama.* Kuala Lumpur: Federal Publications, 1974.

Muhammad Yusoff Hashim (ed.), *Terengganu Daruliman Tradisi Persejarahan Malaysia.* Kuala Lumpur: Dewan Bahasa dan Pustaka, 1991.

Nik Anuar Nik Mahmud, *Tok Janggut: Pejuang atau Penderhaka?* Jabatan Sejarah, Universiti Kebangsaan Malaysia, Bangi, 1999.

Roff, William R., *Kelantan: Religion, Society and Politcs in a Malay State*. Kuala Lumpur: Oxford University Press, 1974.

Rubaidan Siwar, *Pemberontakan Pantai Timur*. Kuala Lumpur: Longman, 1980.

Sa'ad Shukri Haji Muda, *Sejarah Kelantan*. Kota Bahru: Penerbit Kelantan, 1962.

Shaharil Talib, *A History of Kelantan*. Kuala Lumpur: MBRAS, 1995.

Skinner, C., *The Civil War in Kelantan in 1839*, MBRAS, No. 2, 1965.

S. Othman Kelantan, *Perwira*. Penang: Teks Publishing, 1980.

Wells, Carveth, *Six Years in the Malay Jungle*. London: William Heinemann, 1927.

Yahya Abdullah (Y'Abdullah Kelantan), *Peperangan To' Janggut, atau Balasan Derhaka*. Kota Bahru: Muslim Printing Press, 1955.

Articles

A. Rentse, "History of Kelantan", *JMBRAS* 12, pt. 2 (1934): 44–62.

Allen, James de V., "The Kelantan Rising of 1915: Some Thoughts on the Concept of Resistance in British Malayan History", *Journal of Southeast Asian History* 9 (Sept. 1968): 241–57.

Cheah Boon Kheng, "Hunting Down the Rebels in Kelantan, 1915: The Sultan's 'Double Game'", *JMBRAS* 68, pt. 2 (1995): 9–32.

———, "The Romance of To' Janggut, a Kelantan Folk Hero", *JMBRAS* 72, pt. 2 (1999): 49–63.

Ibrahim Nik Mahmood, "The To' Janggut Rebellion of 1915", in *Kelantan: Religion, Society and Politics in a Malay State*, ed. W.R. Roff. Kuala Lumpur: Oxford University Press, 1974, pp. 62–86.

Mohamed b. Nik Mohd. Salleh, "Kelantan in Transition: 1891–1910", in *Kelantan: Religion, Society and Politics in a Malay State*, ed. W.R. Roff. Kuala Lumpur: Oxford University Press, 1974, pp. 22–61.

Mohd. Kamaruzaman A. Rahman, "Perkembangan Ekonomi Kelantan (1900–1920): Peranan Penasihat Inggeris", *Warisan Kelantan* 9 (1990): 44–62.

———, "Penasihat Inggeris, Pembaharuan Pentadbiran Negeri Kelantan dan Pengukuhan Kuasa, 1910–1920", *Warisan Kelantan* 11 (1992): 56–73.

Pepys, W.E., "A Malay Side-Show During the First World War", *Asiatic Review* (Oct. 1950): 1174–9.

———, "Kelantan During World War I", *Malaya in History* 6 (1) (1960).

Tan Ban Teik, "The Tok Janggut Rebellion of 1915 in Kelantan: A Reinterpretation", in *Tokoh-Tokoh Tempatan*, ed. Cheah Boon Kheng. Occasional Paper No. 2, School of Humanities, Universiti Sains Malaysia, Penang, 1982.

Unpublished Manuscripts

Khoo Kay Kim, "The Beginnings of Political Extremism in Malaya, 1915–1935", Ph.D. Thesis in History, University of Malaya, 1973.

Islas @ Ariffin bin Ismail, "Peperangan Tok Janggut, atau Balasan Derhaka, karya Yahya Abdullah (Y. Abdullah): Satu Penilaian", Academic Exercise, History Department, Universiti Sains Malaysia, 1984.

Jones, Alun, "Internal Security in British Malaya, 1895–1942", Ph.D. thesis, History Department, Yale University, New Haven, 1970.

Kassim Ahmad, "Sha'ir Musuh Kelantan", M.A. thesis, University of Malaya, 1961.

Nik Anuar Nik Mahmud, "Sejarah Jeram dan Kebangkitan To' Janggut", B.A. thesis in History, University of Malaya, 1972.

S. Othman Kelantan, "Tok Janggut: Sebuah Citra Pahlawan", Paper presented at "Seminar dan Pameran Perjuangan Tok Janggut", 27–28 August 1996, Kota Bahru.

Index